W9-BNI-802

ALONE!

. . . Suddenly the boat lurched off the bank. Jim lost his balance and pitched into the dark water.

In an instant, the *Evening Star* was above him, its hull within inches of his head. He fought to push himself out from under the boat and surface for air. Then he felt a rope drifting in the water.

Saved! he thought. But the rope uncoiled limply in his hand. It had not been fastened to a deck cleat.

"Help!" he screamed as he began to sink again.

But the muddy water gagged him, and he could not be heard. Neither Ikey far ahead on the towpath nor Dave at the sweep could tell he was not in the bow. He was alone. . . .

CANAL BOY

Karin Clafford Farley

Illustrated by
Dennis Bellile

David C. Cook Publishing Co.
ELGIN, ILLINOIS—WESTON, ONTARIO
FULLERTON, CALIFORNIA

CANAL BOY
Copyright © 1978 David C. Cook Publishing Co.

All rights reserved. Except for brief excerpts for review purposes, no part of this book may be reproduced or used in any form without written permission from the publisher.

Published by David C. Cook Publishing Co., Elgin, IL 60120
Edited by Janet Hoover Thoma

Printed in the United States of America
Library of Congress Catalog Number: 77-94010
ISBN: 0-89191-106-5

CONTENTS

Canal Boy *is the story of two years in the life of James A. Garfield, the twentieth president of the United States. Most of the incidents are based on his diary, his letters and reminiscences, papers of his family and friends, and biographies.*

1

JIM WHAT'S-HIS-NAME

JIM STUMBLED over a rut in the wagon road that led to Orange, a tiny village in northeastern Ohio. Gray shadows hovered around him, making it difficult to see crevices in the uneven dirt. But if he waited for the sun to rise, he would be late for his first day at the salter's.

Why had he stayed up so late last night reading by the light of the fire? Books did not interest him in the morning the way they did at night. Then he could not put them down.

He wanted to lie in the grass beside the road and sleep a little more, but the ground was soaked with dew. How he wished he was walking toward Cleveland to board a clipper ship, instead of walking to the salter's to earn money for his family. But hiring out as a carpenter was still better than farming.

The sun was well up when Jim saw the smoke

that came from the salter's fires. Quickly he jumped a split rail fence and cut across the cornfields.

"Mornin', Mr. Caldwell. I'm ready to begin buildin' your shed if you are still wantin' it," Jim announced as Mr. Caldwell came from behind one of his sheds. The salter's skin and clothes were already dark with smoke and ashes. Jim knew Caldwell burned the wood cleared from farmers' land to make ash.

"I sure need another shed, Jim. We agreed on fifty cents a day for your wages, right?" Caldwell asked to verify the arrangement they had made when he contacted Jim for the job.

"Yeh, that's agreeable with me," Jim answered. But he did not address the older man as "sir." Jim was being hired for his skill, and he never thought of his temporary employers as superiors.

"I saved out some good logs for framin', and I had the mill cut me some boards," Mr. Caldwell explained. "I want the shed built with the sides open—just like the others. Come over this-a-way, and I'll show you where I want it to stand."

As they walked along, Mr. Caldwell bragged, like any merchant who loved his trade. "Potash is one of the biggest exports our country has. France buys a lot just to make glass."

"What do other countries do with it? Make soap?" Jim asked.

"Yeh, soap or fertilizer. I mix the ash with water

in these here big kettles. When the water's steamed off, potash is left. . . . Here, this is where I want the shed." Caldwell pointed to an open space behind the others.

Jim studied the ground, stepping off the footage needed. Then he examined the terrain to see if it was flat enough for footings. Finally he said, "I'll need a shovel to dig postholes first."

"Look in the barn. You'll find whatever you need there. Call me if you want any help," Mr. Caldwell replied as he returned to his work.

Jim measured one of the other sheds to determine the exact dimensions. Then he pounded sticks into the ground to mark where he would put the posts. Now the hard work of digging the postholes, which would serve as a foundation, began. He did not hear a girl almost seventeen, like himself, come up behind him and stop to watch. Finally she said, "Are you the new carpenter my pa hired?"

Jim looked up startled. Then he straightened and took off his hat. "Yes, ma'am. I'm Jim Garfield." Jim thought she had a pretty face but spoiled it by her scowling expression.

"I am Miss Sarah Caldwell," she informed him. "Jim what's-yer-name, dinner is waitin' up at the house. You'd better hurry or we won't save you none." She turned with a swirl of her long skirts and started to walk away. "Wash first!" she added over her shoulders.

Jim put the rye straw hat back on his blond head and picked up his small bundle of clothes. The Caldwells lived in a white clapboard house, not a log cabin like most folks. Once he reached the well out back, Jim brought up a bucket of water and splashed it over his head and arms.

"How's the buildin' goin', Jim?" Mr. Caldwell asked as he joined him.

"I oughta have the posts in by afternoon," Jim replied.

"Good. Come in to dinner now."

Inside the big kitchen, Mr. Caldwell introduced Jim to his wife and three daughters.

"We're glad you're here, Jim. I know your mother," Mrs. Caldwell said. "Sit down now. You must be hungry. After dinner, I'll show you where you'll be sleepin'."

The noon meal was served on china plates instead of the wooden bowls Jim was accustomed to. Mrs. Caldwell encouraged everyone to eat. But when Jim reached for more stew, Sarah gave him such a look of disgust that he changed his mind.

Although Mrs. Caldwell lived in the village of Orange, she was as anxious as most frontier women for news. "How's yer mother?" she asked to begin her inquiries.

"She's well, thank you, ma'am," Jim answered politely.

"My, such a brave widow woman. I've heard tell of how your pa died, and your ma stayed and raised her family. Most folks told her to go back east and start a new life—maybe even catch a husband. But not your ma. She stayed right here."

Jim squirmed. He did not like to hear a recital of his family's troubles. He knew how mother and his older brother, Tom—who was then only eleven—had harvested the crop back in 1833 after pa died. Relatives had helped, but his mother had worked in the fields then, and she still did. What things they couldn't raise or make themselves, mother bartered for, using wool she spun and wove from their sheeps' hair.

"Where are your sisters livin' since they married?" Mrs. Caldwell continued.

"Oh, they both live over in Solon," he answered briefly.

"Does your mother get to see them often?" she asked, looking at her own three daughters.

"Yes, ma'am, mother goes over to stay for a spell, 'specially when there's a new baby." But Jim would not volunteer any more information about his sisters, Hettie Trowbridge and Mary Larebee. Instead he finished his meal quickly so he could get away from Mrs. Caldwell's questions and Sarah's unpleasant glances.

After supper that evening, Jim passed through the parlor on his way to his sleeping place in the attic. As he was about to say good night, he noticed a shelf of books near the chair Mr. Caldwell was sitting in, smoking his pipe. "Can I look at your books, Mr. Caldwell?" he asked hesitantly.

"Can you read, Jim?"

"I can," he answered proudly.

"Sure, you can look at 'em. If you see any you fancy, go ahead and read 'em."

Jim read title after title, maybe more than two dozen books in all—history, arithmetic, biography.

"Can I take one to read tonight?"

"It'll put you to sleep," Mr. Caldwell warned with a laugh.

Jim chose a book about George Washington, the first president. Picking up his candle, he went to his bed under the eaves and began reading.

By the end of the fourth day, Jim pounded the last nail into the roof of the new shed. Then Mr. Caldwell looked at the structure inside and out, nodding his head. Jim had taken great care—digging the postholes deeply and joining the joists of the roof so they met exactly.

"This here is a good piece of work, Jim. You're as good a carpenter as I heard tell," Mr. Caldwell said as he took some money from his pocket. "I said I'd pay you fifty cents a day, and here 'tis." He counted out two dollars in silver coins.

"Thank you, Mr. Caldwell," Jim said, trying to keep from showing how pleased he was.

"I sure could use a hard worker like you to help

me this summer, Jim," the man continued. "I got a big order for potash, and I can't do it alone. Everybody's busy with their own farmin' this time of year. Do you think you could work for me?"

Jim looked down. If he stayed with the salter, he could not get a job on a ship this summer. Mr. Caldwell noticed him hesitate. "I'll pay fourteen dollars a month and room and board," he offered.

Jim looked up. Fourteen dollars a month was good wages. And the Caldwells were nice folks, except for Sarah. Besides, he still had a lot of those books to read.

"I don't know nothin' 'bout makin' potash," Jim said truthfully. "But I'll sure try hard to learn."

"Good!" Mr. Caldwell smiled broadly. "I'll start you out Monday tendin' fires. We want 'em smolderin'. That makes the most ash."

After supper, Jim went up to the attic, anxious to finish a book he had been reading the night before. After a few hours, he finished the last page.

All was silent below. He picked up his candle and went quietly down to the parlor to choose another book. He set the candlestick down so it shone on the books as he studied them.

"What are you doin' here?" shrieked Sarah Caldwell.

Jim turned so fast he knocked the candle over. Quickly he stepped on it so it could not start a fire on the wood floor. Sarah set her candle on the small table by her father's chair.

"You're stealin' somethin', sneakin' down here in the middle of the night when my pa's gone to bed!" she screamed. "Pa! Pa! Come quick."

"I am not stealin'. I was puttin' back a book and gettin' another one. Your pa told me I could read any of the books I wanted to, Sarah!" Jim hollered back.

"Don't you call me Sarah like you was as good as me! You're nothin' but a hired hand. You got no business in our parlor or callin' me by my Christian name. I'm Miss Caldwell to the likes of you." Sarah stood with her hands on her hips as if she were scolding a naughty child.

"What do you mean, 'the likes of me'? You ain't no better or worse than anybody here in Orange. You didn't even go to school!".

"My pa wouldn't send me to that awful school. My ma learned me and my sisters to read and write. Your ma can't read or write. She works in the fields like a man, and you still live in a log cabin instead of a proper house."

Mr. Caldwell rushed into the room, clutching his rifle. "What's goin' on here?"

"I caught Jim what's-his-name sneakin' in here to steal somethin'," cried Sarah.

"I wasn't stealin' nothin', Mr. Caldwell. I was just puttin' back a book I'd finished. You said I could read some books."

"Why are you lettin' a hired hand in our parlor to read our books?" she demanded.

"I caught Jim what's-his-name sneakin' in here to steal somethin'," Sarah cried to her father.

Jim broke in before Mr. Caldwell could reply. "I ain't no thief, and there ain't no disgrace in workin' for somebody for wages. But I ain't no hired hand. We got our own land. We don't have no debts and nobody ever gave us Garfields charity, even when my pa died." Jim stopped to get his breath. "You're a fair man, Mr. Caldwell, but I ain't welcome here. I'm goin' back to my own land, and then I'm walkin' to Cleveland tomorrow to ship out. Nobody calls a sailor a hired hand."

"Now, Jim, just simmer down. Don't pay no mind to an excited girl. You just scared her a mite." Mr. Caldwell put the gun down and moved toward Jim.

"No sir. I'm quittin', and I'm goin' to sea." Jim went up to the attic, picked up his clothes, and ran out into the moonless night.

2

CROPS AND LIVESTOCK

HOW DARE THAT LITTLE SNIP of a girl criticize our family, Jim thought as he stumbled back over the rutted roads toward home. He walked, although he felt like running. After his first fall in the darkness, caution had displaced some of his anger.

He had been less than two years old when his father died, so he had never known him. But he knew his father died caring for his family. Fifteen years ago, when the forest caught fire and flames threatened their cabin, Abram Garfield had fought the fire all day and much of the night. He cut brush, dug ditches, and beat out flames. In the end, he won. The cabin did not burn; there was enough corn and wheat left in the fields so they would not starve that winter.

After he had stamped out the last sparks, he rested in the cool night air. He was black with soot and coughed frequently from the smoke he had breathed so deeply. The next day, he was red with fever. Mother had summoned the only person in the area who called himself a doctor. He applied a blister to father's throat to draw out the poison. Instead, his father got worse. One morning, he left his bed and went to the window to look at his land. Then he turned to his wife. She never forgot his words. "Eliza, I've brought four young saplings into these woods. Take care of them." He returned to bed and died of pneumonia at age thirty-three.

That's why mother had stayed in the Ohio wilderness. When people advised her to parcel her children out to relatives who would raise them to have extra hands to do the work, mother refused. She was small and had never been in good health, but she went out into the woods and began splitting rails. Slowly the fence her husband had begun to protect his fields became longer and longer until the ends finally met. Mother always said she had not kept her family together by her own grit. "Can't do nothin' without the help of the Lord" was her favorite saying.

Jim shifted his packet of belongings to the other shoulder and speeded up his pace. Now he was nearing the creek that flowed through the small clearing his father had hacked out years before. His legs ached from tripping over rocks and ruts, but soon he would be home.

When Jim finally reached the cabin, the latchstring was not out. There was no way to get in except by banging on the door and yelling. The longer he banged, the madder he got.

"It's me, Jim!" he shouted. "You gonna leave me out here all night?" If he had stopped to listen, he would have heard movement inside the cabin. But he was exhausted, and now he felt like an outsider here at home. Finally, Tom opened the door.

"Well, it's about time!" Jim said as he pushed his way into the twenty-by-thirty foot cabin. His mother held a stick into the embers of the fire to light a candle.

"James! What is it? Somethin' terrible happen? What are you doin' home in the middle of the night?" Questions spilled from his mother's lips.

"No more farmin'! No more workin' out for folks as a hired man." He said the last words in a mocking voice. "I'm goin' to sea!" He started up the ladder to collect his things.

Mother stood very still. Only her eyes moved as she looked at Tom, and he looked at her. "James! Get over here. Settle down now," she ordered.

"I'm packin' my stuff, and I'm goin' to Cleveland right now!" Jim yelled back from the loft.

"James! Get down here. I got a right to know why you come bustin' in here in the middle of the night with your dander up," Eliza commanded in a voice she had not used since the boys were small.

Jim appeared at the head of the ladder with a sack and quickly came down.

"Now what's this all about?" she demanded.

"I'm goin', mother. I'll write you from China," Jim said as he started for the door.

"You ain't goin' no place till you tell me what has you so riled up. Now sit down, and I'll make us all some tea."

Tom leaned against the wall near the door. Jim was not going out if his mother did not want him to.

Mrs. Garfield stirred the fire, hung the black kettle on the crane in the fireplace, and pushed it over the flames.

"All right, Jim. What's happened?" she asked as they all sat down at the table. "If you finished at the salter's, why didn't you come home last evenin'?"

Jim told her his story, jumbling the facts in his anger. With quiet, persistent questions, she sorted out his garbled version.

When she did, she was affronted, too, and said so. "Why, who do those Caldwells think they are? Just 'cause they got a white shingled house instead of a cabin? You and Tom are goin' to build us a regular house soon," mother dreamed. But then she added, "Not that it makes any difference. It's what people are, not what they got that counts. I know you gave Caldwell a good day's work for the wages he paid you . . . didn't you?"

"He was so pleased with my work, he asked me to stay on permanent. Offered me fourteen dollars a month and room and board. I said I'd do it. We could use the money to stock up for winter," Jim explained. "But I wasn't no bound boy, no apprentice. I wouldn't call anybody master."

Mrs. Garfield nodded. No boy with folks and land needed to be an apprentice. Jim was a farmer; that was his trade.

Only Jim did not want to be James Garfield, farmer. He wanted to be Captain James Garfield—someday.

"So you see why I quit, mother. I'm sorry about the money, but now I'm goin' to sea. I've put it off too long." Seeing the disapproving look on her face, he continued. "Lots of boys half my age are cabin boys and learnin' about bein' mariners. I gotta go and get caught up."

"And what about us, James? What are Tom and me supposed to do about the crops and livestock?"

"Yeh." Tom's voice was heard for the first time. "You hate farmin' so you think your doin' your share by hirin' out. Well, we cain't afford to hire someone in your place. And mother's gettin' too old to do field work. She has enough to do with weavin' and bakin' and churnin'."

"Tom's right, James. We've tried to make do, but we need you here."

"I only hire out when you don't need me," Jim reminded them.

"Yes, but if you go to sea, you won't be here for the plowin' and harvestin'," Tom argued. "I can't do it alone, and we can't afford a hired hand."

"What about the Boynton boys?" Jim suggested his cousins, who were almost like brothers.

"They got to help their ma and pa. No sir—we got to do our own work like we always done. You can't expect me to go to your Uncle Amos and beg his boys, so you can go off galavantin' to China. Ain't fair, James, not to nobody," his mother asserted. But she could see his jaw was still set in a stubborn line.

"There are things we all wanna do, James. Tom's been wantin' to go to Michigan to try his luck there. He knows of some opportunities, and he's got a right to go before you, 'cause he's nine years older. But he ain't goin' until you and me are taken care of. Obligations come before doin' what we want."

Tom started to agree, but his mother stopped him. It was wise to say no more. "Now it's late, and we gotta get some sleep, especially you, James. Tomorrow is Sunday, and we'll go to meetin'. You pray about it."

Mrs. Garfield rose from the table, and Tom pulled in the latchstring. Then he climbed into the loft. But Jim continued to sit there, drinking his mug of tea and watching the candle burn. As she started toward her bed in the corner, Mrs. Garfield's lips moved, silently praying that he would still be in the cabin in the morning.

Jim put his head down on his arms. He wanted to

be a sailor, but he did not want to desert his family. If he stayed, he would just go on doing the same things every day, every year. No, he had to make himself go to Cleveland, to prove he could take care of himself. But in his mind, Jim could also see great storms at sea, his ship being battered by the wind and waves. He might be washed overboard or the ship might sink and he could be drowned. He knew there was less danger on the Ohio frontier.

His mind flickered back and forth like the candle's flame. He wished someone could help him do what was right. But he could not bring himself to talk to anyone, not his uncle or his cousins. He just could not think anymore. He blew the candle out and climbed into the loft.

3
FREEDOM!

JIM FELT A SHARP PAIN in his ribs, but he could not wake up. Then he felt another. He sat up suddenly, his fist clenched. Tom was laughing at him. "No fightin' on Sunday, baby brother."

"What's the matter with you jabbin' me in the ribs like that?" Jim yelled, reaching for his brother's arm.

But Tom rolled away. "We gotta get the chores done before meetin'. Get up!" Tom pulled on his shirt and trousers and boots and crawled over to the ladder. Just before his shoulders disappeared below the floor of the loft, he reached out and pulled the quilt off Jim's six-foot frame.

"Mornin'," Tom said to his mother, who was stirring meat in the spider, a three-legged frying pan. "Need more wood?"

"Your brother can get it. I hear the cows

moanin'. Go tend to them. . . . James! Get down here. I need more firewood."

"I'm comin', mother," Jim said sleepily from the corner of the loft.

Eliza Garfield poured water she had drawn from the creek into the coffee pot and set it on the irons in the fireplace. She put a loaf of bread and a sharp knife on the table and set out a small tub of the butter she had churned yesterday.

Then she noticed Jim was still not out of the loft. "James! Get down here!"

Soon his feet appeared on the ladder. He did not say anything, but went straight out to the woodpile and began splitting kindling with a short axe.

Tom passed him as he brought a can of fresh, warm milk from the barn and set it on a stone in the creek to cool. Then he picked up the can of milk he had left there the night before and took it into the house.

Soon Jim came in with an armload of wood, which he put in the box near the fireplace. Mrs. Garfield dished meat and potatoes into the wooden bowls and poured coffee and milk into the tin mugs. Then they bowed their heads and clasped hands.

"Dear Lord, thank you for the food we are about to receive and for bringin' us safely to the start of another good day," Mrs. Garfield prayed.

After breakfast, Tom and Jim put on their Sunday clothes, which were not much different from their work clothes. Mother had spun, woven, and stitched them from their own wool. Few people on the Western Reserve frontier had store-bought clothes; folks saved their best homespun for the Lord's Day.

Jim had been to meeting every Sunday of his life. He remembered sitting on his mother's lap when he was small and falling asleep. But as he got older, he listened to the preacher. Sometimes, during the week when nobody was around, he pretended to be a preacher and gave sermons to the trees. He quoted passages from the Bible and explained their meaning. And the trees listened and nodded in the wind, just like people at meeting. The older he was, the more he liked to preach. Next to being a sailor, he would like to be a preacher and tell people about the Lord.

The tiny village of Orange was only a cluster of a few cabins and frame buildings where four or five families lived. But on Sunday, the sparse population for miles around left their isolated homesteads and came there for church—a one-room log building with rough split logs for benches. But people did not come to be entertained. They came from their lonely outposts to have their strength renewed, to be reminded that God would give them courage to meet the exhausting day-in and day-out challenge to keep alive.

Sunday was the one day all week that folks saw others besides their own immediate families. Eliza Garfield always looked forward to seeing her sister, Alpha Boynton, and their other relatives. But today a member of the family from the town of Newburgh was visiting! Thomas Garfield. He looked so much like his brother who had died, that Eliza and Tom were always a little startled when they saw him.

"How's your family, Brother Thomas?" Eliza asked.

"Well, most of them are fine. Ma would have come with me, but she's ailin' a bit. Thought she'd rest today. I got some business interests up in the county that have been keepin' me busy. In fact, that's one of the reasons I came over to Orange today," he added looking at Tom and Jim.

"Oh?" his sister-in-law asked quizzically.

"Well, I got a lumber business up there, and I need men to chop cords of wood for me. I thought to offer the work to Tom or Jim here and Brother Amos Boynton's boys."

"I'm awful busy with the farm now, uncle," Tom replied. "I got a lot of my own choppin' to do to clear more land."

"How about you, Jim? I know you hire out when you're not needed at home. It's June, and the crops are in."

"Well, I got some other things I was plannin' to do, Uncle Thomas. And mother and Tom need me at home," Jim added with slight sarcasm.

"I'm payin' twenty-five dollars for a hundred cord," Uncle Thomas put in.

Twenty-five dollars was twice as much as Jim could have earned at the salter's. And how long would it take to chop some wood? Not long. He could give the twenty-five dollars to his mother and Tom to hire some help. Then he would be free.

Uncle Thomas could see Jim was hesitating. "I'll stop by this afternoon and fetch you in my wagon if you've a mind to go."

Jim nodded in a way that meant neither yes nor no.

As the boys and their mother walked home, Jim tried to determine his mother's feelings. "Do you think I oughta go?" he asked offhandedly.

"Well, you would be finished by harvest time, and it's a lot of money," his mother answered.

"What about hoein' and clearin' like Tom was talkin' about?" he asked to remind them that last night they had said there was too much work at home.

"I guess we could make do, as long as you were home for harvestin'."

June passed. Then so did July, as Jim swung his axe day after day. He had not realized how long it would take to chop a cord of wood. But now he knew. A cord was eight feet long and four feet high.

Each log had to be cut into four-foot lengths. This meant he cut about one hundred four-foot logs for each cord, and he had agreed to cut one hundred cords. Every day men brought wagonloads of freshly cut logs from the forest and dumped them near him.

His only diversion was looking at the lake he would one day sail on. When he rested his axe to wipe the stinging sweat from his eyes, he gazed out on the cool, blue waters of Lake Erie. Sometimes a ship would slide lazily along—its white sails billowed out—and Jim would ache to be out there. He would watch it sail eastward until it slipped over the horizon. Jim thought the ship might be headed for Buffalo, where its cargo would be loaded onto canalboats and towed through the Erie Canal, maybe all the way to the port of New York.

At sundown, he would lay down his axe and walk to the lake to ease his aching muscles and burning hands in the water. The Indians had named this lake the *Erieehronous*. When French fur traders learned that *Erieehronous* meant "cat people"—for those fierce Iroquois who lived on its shore—the French named it *Lac du Chat*. Then the English came. They could not say *Erieehronous,* and it was too long to write on their maps, so they called it Lake Erie.

Now it was August, and Jim was still not through chopping. The summer was slipping away fast; some crops were already being harvested. On

August 15, 1848, his axe fell for the last time. Jim did not take time to survey his work with any satisfaction. He already had the twenty-five dollars in his pocket, since his uncle had paid him two days before. Now that the contract was over; he started for home.

He walked most of the day, arriving at the clearing just before dark. His mother and brother were sitting before the cabin, resting after a long day's work. The look in their eyes told him how much they had accomplished.

Jim hailed them as he stepped out of the long shadows of the forest. "I'm back!" he called.

Tom ran to meet him, slapping him on the back. "Hey, just in time. We got some wood needs choppin', and you bein' a expert now —."

Jim groaned and sank to his knees, pretending exhaustion. "See, mother, no bandages. I got all my fingers and toes. Do you wanna count 'em?" he said jokingly.

"You had your supper yet?"

"Now that you mention it, I am a mite hungry, seein' I just walked fifteen miles."

It was dark now. The three went inside the cabin, and Eliza Garfield put some cold victuals in a bowl and some milk and bread and butter on the table. Jim ate while Tom and mother asked questions about folks at the north end of Cuyahoga County.

When he had eaten, Jim pushed the dishes to

one side and put his hand in his pocket. Then he pulled out the twenty-five dollars. Mrs. Garfield and Tom were silent, then excited, for twenty-five dollars was the most money they had seen at one time for years.

"This is for you and Tom, mother," Jim said as he handed twenty gold pieces to his mother. "I'm keepin' five dollars for myself."

Mrs. Garfield was surprised. Whenever any of them had money, they put all of it in a leather pouch to be used as they needed it. Nobody ever kept any for himself.

Jim knew what his mother was thinking. "I'm goin' to Cleveland in the mornin' to get a job on a ship. I'll need a bit of money till I get paid," he explained quietly.

"Oh, James! I thought you had forgotten that nonsense about bein' a sailor."

"I'll be harvestin' in a few weeks, Jim. I need you," Tom added.

"Twenty dollars will hire a man for forty days," Jim replied.

"Where am I gonna hire an extra hand at harvest time? I gotta work twice as hard. . . ." Tom complained.

"I worked hard, awful hard, choppin' wood fourteen hours a day," Jim shouted back. "Now I'm goin' to sea!"

"James. Listen to me," his mother pleaded. "Don't go to sea. It's a terrible life, and dangerous too. You'll never come back. . . . Please stay here."

"I gotta go, mother. I'm a man, and I gotta do somethin' with my life."

Only Jim was not a man. He was big as a man. He could do a man's work. He could earn a man's wages. But he was not a man in experience, in knowing the ways of the world. Mrs. Garfield and Tom knew this.

"James, you cannot go. Not until you're older."

"I'm goin'. I made up my mind months ago. Now I provided for you, and I'm free to go."

Jim turned and climbed into the loft, picking up a candle as he went. He began assembling the clothes and other things he would need.

In the morning, he climbed down from the loft with his few belongings wrapped in a cloth. He ate breakfast silently. Then his mother packed some food for him, because she knew she could not stop him.

Finally, he stooped to kiss her good-bye. "Don't worry, mother. I can take care of myself. I'm a fightin' boy, ain't I?"

"God protect you, James. I will never stop praying for you."

Jim left the cabin, walked across the clearing, and jumped over the creek, heading northwest toward Cleveland, sixteen miles away.

4

NOT A SAILOR NOR A STEVEDORE

THE ROADS Jim walked that hot, August day were only trails—rough for walking and hardly fit for a man on horseback. Few could accommodate a wagon. The only way to travel the Western Reserve was by water. Moses Cleaveland had done just that when he arrived in 1796 to lay out a plan for the city. Then he departed the way he had come, around the southern shore of Lake Erie and back to the Atlantic seaboard. Not until the Ohio and Erie Canal joined farmers to Eastern markets in 1832 did northeastern Ohio begin to develop. When Jim arrived there in 1848, Cleveland had grown to a city of 10,000.

Axes rang, timbers crashed, and horses, mules, and oxen pulled stumps from the ground as Jim walked out of the wilderness into the dusty Cleveland streets. Even now, thick forests still came up to the very edge of the city. But men, anxious for land, pushed the wilderness farther and farther back.

Instead of going directly to the waterfront, Jim went to Brooklyn Hill, ninety feet above the lake, to study the scene below. Here the coolness of the lake air penetrated a few blocks inland. Jim inhaled its wonderful smell as he looked out over the limitless blue of the lake, so flat and calm on this scorching day. The flats below were lined by two- and three-masted sailing ships and steamships that nestled close to the wharves. Tall lighthouses warned sailors out on the lake that this was Cleveland. Directly below him, the snaking Cuyahoga River meandered out of the wilderness to form Cleveland Harbor. Once a sandbar had blocked its way, and ships had to anchor offshore and row passengers and cargo into land in small boats. But with the coming of the canal, Cleveland's citizens knew the river must connect with the lake; so they dredged a channel to free the Cuyahoga.

They were rewarded by having a harbor crowded with sailing ships and steamers that carried the furs, lumber, wheat, beef, and other products from five states of Wisconsin, Illinois, Michigan, Minnesota, and Ohio to Cleveland, where they were transshipped to canalboats and carried to the eastern states and even Europe. In return the canalboats brought furniture, farm tools, and bolts of cloth to be carried west.

Jim stood on Brooklyn Hill to study the harbor.

As Jim looked at the mouth of the Cuyahoga, he saw lumber scows, grain schooners, tugboats, canalboats, and flatboats. He studied each boat carefully. He had stood on this lofty lookout almost every time he came to Cleveland. But today was different. Before nightfall, he planned to be a member of the crew on one of those boats.

He rejected the steamboats. They relied mostly on steam-driven paddle wheels mounted on each side. They were noisy, belched black smoke, and often blew up. Thousands of people had already been killed in these explosions or had drowned trying to escape the flames as the boats burned to their water lines. Jim also rejected the tugboats and the stubby-ended canalboats. He studied the schooners. This day there were not even many grand schooners in the harbor.

An experienced sailor would have waited a few days for a ship of his liking to arrive. But Jim was neither experienced nor patient. None of the ships were the square riggers of his dreams; in fact, lake ships did not have square rigging. In narrow waters, the vessels had to maneuver frequently and often had to beat against the wind, which required a less cumbersome rigging.

Finally Jim selected the biggest schooner from the forest of masts lining the river. It had only two masts instead of three, but it would do as a start.

When he approached it on the wharf, he began to have some doubts. The ship was old and poorly maintained: its ropes were frayed, its sails graying and tattered, and its paint was peeling everywhere. It did not look like the prosperous merchant ships Jim had read about.

He hesitated. But seeing sailors on the deck, he straightened up, licked his palm, and rubbed it back to smooth his hair. Then he stepped on the gangplank and grinned to think he was boarding a sailing ship.

The two men on deck moved slowly—carelessly—as they coiled rope. It was hot in the harbor basin, and they were doing as little as possible, waiting for the cool of sundown. When they saw the tall, blond farm boy in his homespun clothes and dusty boots, they ignored him.

Jim smiled pleasantly at the first hand he saw. "I'd like to see the captain."

The sailor did not reply.

Jim tried the second man. "I wanna sign on, if you need any more hands," he said, being sure to use the nautical term *sign on* rather than *hire out*, which was landlubbers' language.

Both sailors began snickering. "You'd be wantin' to see the cap'n then," said the second hand, bursting into laughter as he finished the sentence.

At that moment Jim heard a voice roaring up from an open hatch. Soon a huge, dirty man dragged himself up on deck and stood there reeling. He continued to rage at some hapless person or thing below. But he was so drunk, his speech was thick and unintelligible. Jim felt like he had been hit over the head and punched in the stomach at the same time. This man was obviously the captain the way he shouted orders. All Jim's images of the stalwart, brave, and gallant vessel masters he had read about were swept away.

Jim wanted to run across the deck and down the gangplank, but he would not let himself. If this was part of sea life, so be it. He stepped forward.

"Captain? My name is Jim Garfield from Orange. I wanna sign on as a hand if you're needin' anybody. I got some experience floatin' lumber down the canal, and I'd—"

The drunken captain turned all his anger on Jim. He did not answer Jim's question; instead he cursed him with words the boy had never heard before. Although Jim had been brought up by his mother, he had worked among men for five years. But the toughest and wildest frontiersmen and half-breeds had never talked like this.

Jim turned and walked down the gangplank and along the wharf. The laughter and jeers of the deck hands followed him. He walked fast, but he would not run.

Finally he reached the end of a long wharf and could go no further. The sounds of the sailors' laughter echoed through his mind. He thought about jumping off the pier into the muddy waters. He wanted to wash off the filthy language that had been spit on him. But Jim was angry at himself, too. Why had he let them bluff him off that ship? Why had he not thrown at least one of them over the side?

He sat down on a piling, because he had nowhere else to go. All around him commerce flowed, totally ignoring the frontier boy. The stevedores, who only loaded and unloaded ships, rolled barrels up the gangplanks. Sailors repaired canvas, high in the rigging of their ships. Well-dressed merchants argued prices with homespun farmers over wagon loads of produce. Jim did not belong here. He was not a sailor nor a stevedore, and certainly not a merchant. Maybe he should hitch a ride home in a farmer's empty wagon.

But he could not go home now, not after only one day. As the sun went down, the merchants closed their warehouses. Cooks on board the ships rang bells to call sailors out of the rigging to the evening meal below deck. The farmers had long since started home. Still Jim sat on the wharf, staring at the ever-moving water.

5

EVEN AN OVERGROWN ROWBOAT

THE AUGUST NIGHT stayed warm, so Jim curled up in an outside corner of a warehouse, resting his head on his belongings. He was awakened early the next morning by the screaming of lake gulls as they rose from their nesting places and dipped and dived in search of food. After finishing the last of the bread and cheese his mother had packed for him, Jim walked along the docks, careful to stay away from the ship he had visited. He wanted to inquire about work, but he could not bring himself to walk up another gangplank.

Finally he left the waterfront and went into the streets of the town. Cleveland was expanding so fast he knew there would be work for a carpenter. He walked past lumber yards, mercantile houses, iron foundries, candle and soap factories, breweries, carriage works, and potteries. These businesses crowded as close to the river as possible, on a first come, first serve basis.

Eventually Jim found himself on Superior Street. As he strolled down this broad thoroughfare—which did not have sidewalks or cobblestone paving yet—the city became more like a large country town. He saw the courthouse, with its whipping post and pillories in front, the churches, and the fine brick and stone houses set on generous pieces of land. Jim wondered what it would be like to live in a house that was twenty times the size of his cabin home. The mother of the house—or more likely servants—cooked on stoves instead of open fireplaces. He wondered if the cooks fought to keep the cockroaches and mice away from the food like his mother did.

He reached the large square Moses Cleaveland had scratched out with his sword. It was wooded and cool. Jim sat down on the grass and watched the wagons rumble by. Now and then he glimpsed fancy carriages that rolled southeast on Euclid Avenue toward the fine homes. He watched ladies and gentlemen in store-bought clothes go in and out of shops and banks that faced the square. Cleveland would be a fine place to live.

But then Jim remembered he did not want to be a carpenter. He could do that back in Orange. He wanted to sail on a ship. After yesterday, he would settle for any kind of boat, even an overgrown rowboat like a bateau. Sitting on the ground in the Cleveland square, he prayed he might find a place on a ship—any ship.

He stood up and walked over to Clair Street, down the steep bluff, and back onto the waterfront. How much he had learned in one day; yesterday he had thought it would be easy to hire on a boat. Now he would have to risk another rejection, maybe a lot of them. He knew one thing: he would not go home.

Thinking about home made him remember that his cousin, Amos Letcher, had a boat on the Ohio and Erie Canal. If Jim could find him, Amos might know of a job.

Jim began to question the men who worked the canalboats.

"Do you know a cap'n name of Amos Letcher?"

Canallers, or "canawlers," as they called themselves, were different from lake sailors or seamen. They were a semivagaband people who lived and fought hard. Those who drifted up and down the 4,000 miles of canals from New York State to Illinois numbered in the thousands, so canallers could live among their own. They were suspicious of anyone else. Land people in turn only tolerated canallers for the prosperity they brought. They hated their brawling, stealing, and depravity.

Canallers being canallers, Jim was not given any answers to his question, only "Heard of him."

After that the canallers said no more, and the look on their faces defied him to ask further.

Only the captain of a canal packet boat, which carried passengers, would give Jim any directions. "Saw the *Evening Star* taking on copper ore from a schooner in from Lake Superior. Look up there," he replied as he stood on the deck greeting passengers. He waved his hand upriver and then disappeared inside the cabin.

At least Jim learned the name of Amos Letcher's boat. He had only seen him a few times, so he was not sure he would recognize him. Now Jim walked along quickly, looking at the name on every canalboat he passed. The captain had been so vague in his directions, Jim was not sure he was going in the right direction.

"Have you seen the *Evening Star?*" he asked a passerby. "Cap'n Letcher's boat?" The man shrugged his shoulders and moved on.

Maybe the *Evening Star* had started up the canal again. Maybe the packet boat captain saw it yesterday, Jim fretted.

He sat down on a coil of rope to think. He had been walking up and down all day, so he closed his eyes for a few minutes.

"You lookin' for me, young feller?"

Jim looked up and saw a powerful man, perhaps ten years older than he, standing in front of him. The man's hard blue eyes looked into Jim's suspiciously.

"I heard you been askin' round. I'm Amos Letcher."

Jim jumped up. "Amos Letcher! Yes, sir. I sure have been ahuntin' you."

"You bringin' word from my family. Somethin' wrong back on the farm?" Letcher asked, assuming from Jim's appearance that he was not from the canal or the town.

Jim smiled. "Oh, no. I'm Jim Garfield. Been a long time since you seen me. I guess you don't remember me."

"Jim Garfield," Amos Letcher said slowly as he scratched his beard and studied Jim's face. He sorted out his relatives on his mother's side. Finally he said, "You be Uncle Abram's boy from over t' Orange?"

"Yes, sir," Jim answered, happy to be remembered.

"You got a older brother and some sisters?" Amos recalled.

"That's right, Cap'n Letcher, and my mother."

"Good woman, your ma. God-fearin' woman." He seemed to think more of Aunt Eliza Garfield than she thought of him. Jim remembered that his mother thought Amos was a renegade—a farm boy whose family worked the farm while he was off "galavantin' up 'n down the canal."

"What you doin' here in Cleveland, Jim?" he asked in a friendly manner, now that Jim was kinfolk.

"I come to be a sailor, Cap'n Letcher. Farmin's not for me."

Amos Letcher restrained a sad smile. He had heard words like that from other young farm boys and often with tragic results.

Jim rushed on. "I tried to sign on a schooner yesterday, but they laughed me off. I told 'em I had experience takin' lumber down the canal. Anyway," Jim finished lamely, "I thought you might know of some boat that needed a hand."

"Well, Jim, I need a hoggee, but I don't think you'd be interested if you got your mind set on a lake schooner," Amos Letcher said tentatively.

Jim was disappointed. A hoggee was the lowest position on the canal; he drove the horses along the towpath, pulling the boat through the water. *Drivin' those horses will be a lot like plowin' back on the farm,* he thought.

But he said, "The way I figure, cap'n, I gotta learn the sailin' business somehow. If you'd be willin' to take me on, I'd try my darndest to do the job."

"I'm leavin' in a hour up the canawl t' Akron, then takin' the Crosscut Canawl to the Ohio River and over to Pittsburgh. You can try it for one trip," Letcher explained. "Maybe when you get back, you can find a lake boat that'll take you on. Pays twelve dollars a month and your keep."

Well, I ain't never been to Pittsburgh. Ain't been any place more'n twenty miles from Orange, Jim thought and held out his hand. "I'd be proud to learn canallin' from you, Cap'n Letcher."

Letcher shook his hand with a powerful grasp and said seriously, "You'll learn a lot, Jim. Maybe more'n you wanna learn."

6

ISN'T LIKE PLOWING!

A SMALL STEAM TUGBOAT towed the *Evening Star* two miles up the Cuyahoga River to the foot of Superior Street, where the first lock, No. 42, would lift it above the level of Lake Erie. Someone handed Jim a long setting pole and told him to push hard against the river bottom. Captain Letcher, the cook, two steersmen, the bowman, and the other hoggee all grabbed setting poles, and slowly the *Evening Star* moved toward the lock chamber.

Jim was sure the boat would tear apart against the sides of the chamber, which was only fifteen to twenty feet wide and ninety feet long. But the crew nosed the clumsy boat carefully into the lock, with only five feet to spare. Then the gate creaked slowly shut, and the sluice gates in the bottom of the upstream end opened to allow the water to flow in. Quickly the crew threw lines around the lock's four snubbing posts to hold the boat steady. As the rushing water moved the boat upward, the ropes had to be raised to higher posts along the wall.

Each time the ropes were moved, the surging water forced the *Evening Star* dangerously close to the chamber's rough stone walls. Again Jim thought the boat's wooden sides would be torn away. Within an hour of signing on as a crew member, Jim found that canalling was hard and dangerous work.

Finally the water raised the canalboat ten feet, the front gate swung all the way open, and the crew poled the *Evening Star* into the canal basin at the foot of Seneca Street. Jim turned to look back at the panoramic view of men and machinery that powered the canal. Locking through that mechanism had only taken ten minutes.

Now the boat was in the lock cradle, where it was weighed and certified to be carrying fifty tons of iron ore. Tolls were charged according to the boat's weight and the number of miles it would be traveling on the canal. While Captain Letcher paid his fees and had the papers stamped to show lockkeepers along the canal, Jim had his first chance to look at his new home.

The *Evening Star* was a long boat of eighty-five feet, but shallow, only two or three feet deep. The steersman guided the boat by a long, heavy tiller attached to a large rudder that protruded from the back of the boat. The front of the *Evening Star* was high and rounded. Two shacks rose above the boat's sides. One was the cook's shack, where food was prepared and the crew slept when they were not working. The other shack, located just back of the bow, housed the horses that towed the boat. Each canalboat kept two teams of horses or mules and two drivers.

Being a freighter, the *Evening Star* was not brightly painted like a passenger packet boat. In fact, it was in need of paint and repairs, because the boat had been in constant use since April. Repairs were only made during the three to five months the canals froze over or the weeks they ran dry. Otherwise, canalboats moved twenty-four hours a day, seven days a week. A boat that did not, lost money for its owners.

Soon the other hoggee, Ikey—a boy about Jim's age, began to show Jim how to hitch and drive the team.

"You gotta hitch the horses one in front of the other. Walkin' the towpath ain't like plowin'," he explained.

Jim nodded that he understood.

"Now you gotta keep the towline tight, so the *Star* will move right smart. But you gotta watch. Other boats will be comin', or the steersman will have to get around the shanty boats or them dang cribs." Ikey spat disgustedly on the ground as if to spit on the slow-moving timber rafts and house-boats that clogged canal traffic. They were obstacles for the steersmen and their hoggees.

"Now the cap'n's gonna yell at you, 'You're goin' too slow!' or 'Slow down, you're goin' too fast!' And the steersman is gonna yell at you, and the bow-man is gonna yell, too. But bein' sixty feet up this here towpath, you cain't hear 'em good, so you gotta just look sharp and do what you think you gotta. Don't pay too much mind to them yellin' from the *Star*."

Jim was beginning to see that being a hoggee was not so easy, and he wondered how Ikey did it. Although he was tall, he was thin and spindly. His hair was dark, and his skin tan. Yet to Jim, he looked like he might not get enough to eat.

Ikey continued, "Now the only one not yellin' at you is the cook. Always be nice to cooks, 'cause if you do, they save food for you when you come off your shift. And they let you warm up by the stove if it's cold or been rainin' and give you food to eat while you're drivin'."

Jim nodded when Ikey paused to see if he had any questions. Then Ikey went on.

"Each of us drive for six hours. When you're through, be sure to rub down your team good and look 'em over for sores. Cap'n don't want no sick horses. Check the harness real good. Cain't have no broken harness, makin' the *Star* have to stop."

Captain Letcher came out of the toll collector's

shack and jumped aboard the *Evening Star*. "Deadeye!" he ordered. A deckman quickly fastened the thick towline to a T-shaped cleat called the deadeye, in the middle of the boat.

"Ready, you hoggee?" he called to Jim and Ikey up the towpath.

Jim grasped the reins firmly, and Ikey called back, "Aye, sir!"

"Cast off!" Captain Letcher yelled. A wharfman loosened the mooring hawsers from the snubbing posts on the dock and threw them onto the deck.

"Now!" ordered Ikey.

Jim slapped the reins on the horses' backs, stirring them to a slow walk. The towline stretched tight, and the canalboat began moving silently through the water.

Ikey walked beside Jim, giving advice. "Now you gotta talk nice to Kit and Nance here. They'll do what you want, but you gotta be nice to 'em. When you get tired of walkin', Kit here, in the back, will let you ride her. She's the lean horse and the most important—and she knows it. Keep her stall real clean, 'cause her stall is the best one for sleepin' in."

"We sleep with the horses?" Jim asked, thinking of his bed in the loft at home.

"You can sleep on deck if you wanna, but I once got kicked into the canawl by a cap'n doin' that," relayed Ikey matter-of-factly.

"Cap'n Letcher pushed you in the canal? What

did he do that for?" Jim was surprised at this cruel side of his cousin.

"Oh, no, not Cap'n Letcher."

Jim was relieved.

"Cap'n Letcher's tough. Ain't nobody on the canawl he cain't beat up. But he's fair. He keeps his word. This is my second year workin' for him. T'weren't Cap'n Letcher kicked me in the canawl."

"Why did that other captain push you in anyway?"

"I didn't say pushed, I said kicked." Ikey put a hand on his back, as if he could still feel the pain. "Broke a couple of ribs doin' it."

"Why?" Jim repeated.

" 'Twas gettin' to the end of the season, and he didn't wanna pay me my wages. Captains don't pay the hoggees till the canawl freezes over. If they don't wanna pay you, they're mean to you so you run away," said Ikey.

"That's not fair!" Jim protested.

"Another time I got the fever and couldn't work. I was clean outta my head and burnin' up. I fell down on the towpath. Cap'n just left me there in the sun and had the other fellow drive the team. Laid there half a day, flies crawlin' all over me. Next hoggee came along and dragged me outta the way of his team."

"He didn't stop to help you?"

"He hadda keep drivin'. Cain't stop for nothin'," Ikey explained with a shrug.

"Somebody musta helped you," Jim said.

"Oh, a nice fella from the mission society came along and took me home. His wife nursed me. I stayed all winter with 'em. I was sure too weak to move for a long time. The mission society folks are always helpin' the hoggees. Some of these little kids are only eleven or twelve. They need a lotta help. The mission fellow got me this job with Cap'n Letcher. Sure am obliged to him."

"Don't you have no kinfolk?" Jim asked, wondering why Ikey's family had not nursed him.

"My ma and pa died back in the Great Sickness of '32, when I was just a baby. Some neighbor folks raised me. But they had a lotta kids of their own, and I was sorta takin' food from them. So I heard about good jobs on the canal, and I come lookin' for one."

Jim thanked God he had a family.

The bowman sounded his horn. "Boat ahead!" he called out.

"Hold the line steady!" Dave, the steersman, yelled from the back of the boat.

Jim was startled. He had forgotten to watch the team and the towrope. But Kit and Nance had seemed to know what to do without much help from him.

Dave was maneuvering the *Evening Star* to the far side of the forty-foot wide canal to avoid an oncoming boat that had the right-of-way.

"Stop the team! Get 'em over to the outside of the

towpath. Let the line go slack in the water," Ikey instructed Jim. The towpath was only ten feet wide with a wall of forest beside it. There was not much room to move over. "Their team and boat gotta pass over our line. We gotta stop to let 'em!"

"Hold the line, damn you!" Dave yelled again.

In his confusion, Jim pulled on the reins hard and fast. The horses, unused to this new driver, bolted and snapped the towline taut. Jim tripped on it and went head first into the muddy canal waters, just two feet below the towpath.

Jim had never learned to swim. Although the canal was only four feet deep, Jim could not get his footing to stand up. The weeds on the slippery bottom entangled his feet. He thrashed about and once disappeared below the surface.

But Ikey could not help him. The other boat's horses were coming toward him. If he left their team, the two lines could become hopelessly entangled. One or both of the teams might be dragged into the canal where Jim was floundering.

Quickly Captain Letcher grabbed a long setting pole and held it out to Jim. But he was blinded by the water in his eyes and could not see it. The other canalboat was bearing down on him.

"Grab the pole!" Captain Letcher and the crew yelled at him.

Finally Letcher managed to shove it into his ribs. "Grab it now! Cain't you feel it?"

Jim grabbed on before it pushed him under

again. Then Letcher and Dave pulled Jim out of the way of the oncoming boat. They dragged him over the *Evening Star's* low side. Coughing to clear his lungs of the muddy water, Jim tried to thank them. But no one had time to listen.

The *Evening Star* had to move again. "Sound the horn!" Captain Letcher ordered. The bowman blew the piercing sound that could be heard a long way off.

Immediately Ikey started the horses on their slow, plodding way. Captain Letcher and cook manned setting poles to keep the boat from becoming stuck fast to the canal's side, while Dave maneuvered the long steering sweep to guide the boat into midstream.

Only when the *Evening Star* was moving smoothly through the water did anyone have time for Jim. He still sat on the deck, his head down. "I'm sorry, cap'n," he said, careful not to call Amos Letcher cousin.

"Sure, Jim. Anybody can take a spill from that slippery path. Happens to experts. This is only your first day." Amos Letcher tried to excuse him. "You'll learn the ways of the canawl. After all, your pa dug it," he reminded Jim.

Though he was wet and miserable, Jim wanted to hear more about his father and the canal. His mother had always refused to speak about it.

"What part did he dig, cap'n? Do you know?" Jim asked.

"Was down in Tuscarawas County near Newcomerstown back in 1825 or '26. Your pa had big ideas about not bein' a farmer. He wanted to be a canawl contractor and make lots of money. Had canawl fever like most folks in Ohio—like most folks in the United States, I reckon. Everybody wanted canawls for gettin' rich quick like the folks in New York State did."

"How big a section did he dig?" Jim wondered.

"Not much," Captain Letcher shook his head sadly. "When the canawl was bein' built, a feller could contract to dig one half mile. He hadda hire about twenty laborers—feed 'em, house 'em, give 'em tools. Well, your pa got a crew together, built a cabin, and your ma cooked three big meals a day. But then they ran into trouble diggin', and prices started goin' up. Your pa lost money. Finally he got the ague, and so did your ma. They lost everything. They was so sick, kinfolks took 'em in for a couple of years."

"A couple of *years?*" Jim repeated, finding this hard to believe of his small but strong mother.

"Oh, every harvesttime, 'specially, they'd get the fever real bad. Finally your pa came around. Your ma talked him into goin' back to farmin'. It was somethin' a family could depend on. They went up to Orange with Uncle Amos Boynton and bought eighty acres. Your pa started clearin' it. But he didn't last long."

Jim started to ask another question, but Letcher

saw he was beginning to shiver. "Go inside the shack and get some dry clothes. Cook will give you some coffee. Cain't have no drivers sick."

"Yes, sir," Jim answered. "I'll get dry right away. But I'll finish my shift on the path till it's time for Ikey to take over. Sure am obliged to Ikey for holdin' the team when I fell in."

"Ikey cain't always be there, Jim. Watch out on the path. It's a mighty dangerous place. You're up there alone. Lines get tangled, the path's slipperier than a eel. Smart alecks from the town wait in hidin' along the towpath just to beat up the hoggees for fun," the captain warned sternly. "We gotta keep movin'. If you're gonna be a canawller, you gotta be able to take care of yourself and the *Evenin' Star*. If you cain't, the companies find out, and we don't get no more business."

Jim understood. "Back home, I was called a fightin' boy," he replied.

Letcher looked him over. "Maybe," he said.

7

NO PLACE FOR COWARDS

AFTER JIM FINISHED his shift, he brought Kit and Nance on board and watered and curried them carefully, talking in a soft voice. He stroked them, so the animals would come to know him as their friend.

After they were bedded down, Jim sat on the deck by a running light inspecting the harness. It had been a long but exciting day. Sitting there on the deck, he felt like a member of the crew. He was a sailor—or at least a canaller.

He thought of his mother's and Tom's faces when he would bring his wages home after the canal closed for the winter. His mother could buy so many things with the money. In fact, since he was going to a big town like Pittsburgh, he might buy her a pretty length of calico. Then she could make herself a dress of fancy, printed material rather than homespun. He smiled to himself. He might not be on a schooner or on Lake Erie, but at least he was moving through the water under the stars.

Suddenly the bowman's horn sounded.

"Johnny Cake Lock ahead!" he shouted.

Just as the lock's bright lanterns became visible, Jim heard the sound of another horn, followed by shouting. Captain Letcher appeared on deck. "Dave! Get up here," he ordered. Then he went to the bow. "Bowman, make ready the lock!"

"Other boat says they're ready to enter," the bowman shouted back.

"So are we!" Letcher answered. "Be the other boat a packet, then she has the right of way. Be she not, we're first in the lock. Tell 'em Letcher says so!" he demanded. "And tell that lockkeeper to let the water down or I'll drown him in his own lock!"

"Only the lockkeeper's helper's here. Lockkeeper went home to sleep. Didn't expect many boats tonight," the bowman answered.

Letcher groaned. When the lockkeeper was not at the lock, there was no one to settle disputes, and time was lost. "Why don't the danged canawl company hire more lockkeepers? No man can work twenty-four hours a day," the captain muttered.

Dave and the other steersman had come on deck with clubs, which seemed to be kept for such occasions. Cook appeared with the long knife used to cut towropes.

"Jim! Git up on the towpath and help Ikey. Try to cut their towrope with this." Letcher handed Jim the huge, wicked-looking knife.

"Wait a minute, cap'n. I was out on deck. The other boat was at the lock first and besides they're comin' downstream. They have the right. . . . Anyway, the water is up. They can go in, and when the water is down, it'll be level with us. That'll save time for both boats."

Captain Letcher was so startled to have his newest crew member tell him what to do that he did not hit Jim. Instead, he explained. "When two boats meet at a lock, they always fight over who oughta be first. If the lockkeeper cain't settle it, best crew wins."

"Come on, cap'n, we're wastin' time talkin' to this kid. If he's afraid to fight, we don't need him," Dave said impatiently.

By this time, taunts from the other crew could be heard across the lock. Dave and the other steersman started for the towpath.

"Wait!" Captain Letcher commanded. "It'll only take a few minutes for them to go through the lock. A fight would take a lot longer. We got a contract to get this ore to Pittsburgh, and I'm short of crew. Cain't spare nobody to be laid up from fightin'."

"Bowman!" he shouted. "They can have the lock first. Stand by."

"Cap'n!" Dave said. "You cain't not fight 'em. We can win, short-handed or not. Ain't you and me the best fighters on the canawl? We got a reputation to uphold. If we don't fight, every pirate on the canawl will be after us. We'll be known as an easy mark!"

Dave was in his thirties and had been known as the best fighter for almost twenty years. He was also the best steersman and the best paid and most important person on the boat except for the captain.

"You wanna fight it out with me, Dave? Who gives orders on this here boat?"

Instead of fighting the captain, Dave turned on Jim. "You baby-faced coward. You go back to the farm and your mama. Cain't be a canawler unless you're a fighter. No place for cowards on the canawl. Get off, or you'll find yourself floatin' in it some night," he threatened as the crew grumbled their agreement.

"I'll decide who works on the *Star* and who don't," Captain Letcher yelled, pulling attention back to himself. "If Jim's a coward, he'll be the first of his name that ever was. Back to your posts," he ordered.

The lock slowly inched open as the high water poured out, making a whirlpool in front of the gates. The other boat emerged on the low water and headed for Cleveland. Jim thought the other crew would appreciate Letcher's courtesy. Instead they insulted him, calling him and his crew cowards and worse—far worse than Dave had called

Jim when he suggested they wait.

But there was little time to worry. The Portage Summit Cascade started after this lock. The next twenty locks would be stairsteps—one right after the other—lifting the *Evening Star* to Akron.

Now the team was unhitched and brought aboard. Everyone manned setting poles and poled the canalboat into each lock. Then they strained to hold the ropes steady, keeping the *Star* centered in the lock. Only lanterns lit the shadowy walls and murky waters. When the upstream end opened, they poled into the next lock. This tense, exhausting process was repeated over and over throughout the night.

But no one talked to Jim except the captain; even Ikey turned away. Cowards could not survive on the canal. Jim had spoken up for fair play. But there was no justice here, just trickery from canallers and land people alike. Now he was alone.

At Akron, the *Evening Star* turned directly east into the Ohio and Pennsylvania Canal. This canal was called the Crosscut because it cut into the Ohio and Erie Canal to form a direct waterway to Pittsburgh.

From midnight until six in the morning and from noon to six at night, Jim walked the towpath with Kit and Nance. These were not the good shifts, but Ikey had seniority. Jim worked without complaining. As the teams changed every six hours, he tried to resume their earlier friendship.

But Ikey rarely responded. Jim kept Kit's stall clean so Ikey could sleep there, but Ikey did not return the favor.

Jim slept out on deck most nights. He figured his cousin would not kick him off, but he was not sure about Dave and the others. Once when he fell into the canal again, Dave helped pull him out. But Captain Letcher had been there. If the captain hadn't been around, Jim knew Dave would have let him drown.

When the *Evening Star* passed through Warren, Ohio, Jim saw a medicine showboat tied up along the canal bank. A dancing bear was entertaining a knot of town folks. The boat was colorfully painted, with signs all over it. One advertised a fortune teller who would reveal the rest of your life if you gave her a silver coin. Jim wished he could stop and ask her if he would ever get on a schooner or see China?

As soon as a large crowd had gathered, a medicine man came out of the cabin and began describing the advantages of his remedies.

"This elixir is the latest discovery, coming directly to you from the great medical center at Vienna, Austria. That's in Europe, folks," he stopped to explain and then continued. "It was discovered by the world's greatest doctors! The Queen of England paid hundreds of dollars for it to cure her melancholia. . . . It will cure your ague, headaches, backaches, club feet, fits, and insanity. Think of it.

One dollar to feel good!"

Evidently many people believed him, because they began buying the remedy. People tried anything—boiled bark, crushed berries, bags of herbs around their necks—to bring relief to their many illnesses.

Mebbe this medicine from Europe would have saved pa, Jim speculated. *If it hadda been invented back then.*

Jim was in front with the team when Nance threw a shoe near the little town of Niles. He halted the horses and went back to notify the captain.

After swearing at the delay for a few minutes, Letcher ordered Jim to unhitch the team. "Take Nance and go ahead into town to find a blacksmith. Ikey's team will pull the boat. When the shoe's fixed, catch up with us."

As Jim led the limping horse along the towpath, he was spotted by two little boys fishing with sticks and string on the berm side of the canal, the bank opposite the towpath. Quickly they pulled their fishing lines up and ran across the low bridge.

" 'Lo, hoggee," they said.

Jim tried to look important, because these children obviously admired canal drivers.

"Where you goin'?" one asked.

"Why's your horse limpin'?" the other added.

"Gotta get my horse's shoe fixed," Jim answered.

When a large crowd had gathered, a medicine man appeared to describe his elixir.

"I can take you to the blacksmith," the sturdy towheaded boy volunteered importantly. "Follow me!"

Jim smiled as this mite marched ahead, his fishing pole over his shoulder like a parade marshal. Jim followed leading Nance, and the other fisherman trudged behind.

Niles was a small mill town. Sparks flew from sheds that made tire and sheet iron, judging by the products stacked outside. Coal, which was mined nearby, was piled everywhere.

The little boy marched Jim down the dusty main street to a large blacksmith shop. Inside, he addressed a huge, gray-haired man.

"Mr. Burton, this driver's from the *canal.*" He emphasized the final word. "Needs a new shoe for his horse."

The blacksmith, who had scars from old burns all over his bare, sooty arms, bowed to the child. "Does he now, Willie? I thank ye for bringin' him to me shop," he said in the thick accent of a man born in Wales.

"Do a good job for him," the child instructed the blacksmith.

"Yes sir," he answered, laughing.

The boy turned to Jim. "While Mr. Burton is fixin' your horse, my pa's store is across the street, in case you're needin' anything for you or your boat."

Jim was amused by the child's enterprise, and

later by his confidence as he guided Jim around this town that had prospered from canal business. Boats brought iron ore here to be forged over the coal mined locally. Besides his father's large general store, there were several others and a bank. Everywhere Jim heard the same brogue.

When the horse was shod, Willie led Jim back to the towpath. Willie's friend had tired of the tour long ago and had gone home.

"Much obliged to you," Jim said as he mounted Nance bareback. "What did you say your name was?"

The child drew himself up like a soldier answering roll call. "William McKinley."

"Mine's Jim Garfield. Maybe I'll see you when I come back this way from Pittsburgh," he said, hoping the child was impressed.

"Bye," Willie answered, and he waved his small hand until Jim was out of sight up the towpath.

8

STREET LIGHTS AND RUNNING WATER

ALL CANALBOATS STOPPED at nine in the morning and two in the afternoon so food could be cooked and the horses and mules allowed to graze. No fires could be lit while the boat was moving. The danger of an accident and the loss of cargo was too great.

If another team was close by during this break, Jim talked to the hoggee. If this was also his first year on the canal, he replied quite openly. But an experienced boy often realized Jim was new and started a fight. Jim could not understand why. But he gave them what they asked for.

After two fights, Jim learned to maneuver his opponent onto the grass rather than roll in the horse manure that littered the towpath. Jim usually won but not without a bloody nose or split lip.

One older hoggee seemed to want to talk. "Where you from?" he asked.

"We're outta Cleveland," Jim answered, trying

to sound like an experienced canaller. "Where you from yourself?"

" 'Round."

Jim knew this meant he was a runaway. Runaways never said where they were from, because many had been apprentices, or indentured boys, and could be returned to their masters until they were twenty-one. These boys became lost among the canallers and moved quickly from place to place with their boats, avoiding those who hunted them.

After a few more questions, the hoggee turned his back on his boat and pulled a bottle of whiskey from under his shirt.

"Wanna swig?" he said in a friendly way.

To refuse would have been enough insult to start a fight, so Jim took the bottle and pretended to drink.

"Good stuff, huh?" the boy said. "Stole it off the steersman last night. He bought two bottles at the lockkeeper's dram shop day before yesterday. He drank the other one and passed out before he could finish this one."

"You stole it off another crew member?"

"Sure. When I'm a steersman makin' twenty silver dollars a month, I won't have to steal. But till then—" He lifted the bottle in salute and drank a big gulp.

"What you gonna do when the steersman finds out it's gone?" Jim asked, thinking of Dave.

"Tell him he threw it in the canal after he finished it. He thinks he's a two-bottle man, but he ain't. I done it before," the boy bragged. "Say, you got any money on you?"

"A little," Jim replied cautiously.

"Well, I noticed—if you don't mind me sayin' so—you only got rope holdin' your pants up. Hoggees like you and me need a good belt buckle."

"Why?"

"For fightin', of course. Ain't you ever had a couple of town toughs jump you on the path, especially when you was 'round the bend, outta sight of your boat?"

Jim shook his head.

"Well, boy, I have. But you just whip off a belt with a buckle like this and swing it 'round and 'round. You can hold off five or more. In fact, I once drove a bunch of 'em right into the canawl. Just like herdin' cows." The boy laughed and slapped his knee. "I got an extra buckle right here. Always keep two buckles, in case I lose one in a fight." Then he added with a smile on his face, "But you're a nice fella. New to the canawl, ain't you?"

Jim nodded reluctantly.

"You need a buckle."

"How much?" Jim asked.

"How much you got?"

"I don't need a belt buckle. I ain't got a belt," Jim reminded him.

"Aw, you can get a belt cheap from a peddler's

boat or a cobbler in any town," persuaded the boy.

"Thanks a lot, but I gotta eat now. Cook don't like to be kept waitin'." He started to walk away. "Thanks for the drink. Real friendly of you."

As Jim turned around, a heavy wallop hit the back of his neck. He fell forward on his knees. The other boy jumped on him, pinning him down.

"I asked real nice," he said fiercely. "Now gimme your money. All of it!"

Jim was stunned. The boy started going through his pockets. As his head cleared, he pretended to still be semiconscious. The boy released his tight grip to search him. Jim waited until the right time, then he bolted and threw the boy off balance. Now Jim was the one on top. He hit the thief hard. Then he reached into the other fellow's shirt, took the whiskey bottle out, and hurled it into the canal. The boy lay in the grass as Jim walked back to the boat.

Soon the *Evening Star* went through Youngstown and at Newcastle passed into the Pennsylvania Canal. But canal traffic increased little, because the area above Newcastle did little business. Jim and Ikey took turns driving the horses until the boat entered the canal basin at Beaver—or old Fort McIntosh, as some frontiersmen still called it. The crew waited impatiently while Captain Letcher hired a steamer to pull the *Evening Star* up the Ohio River to Pittsburgh.

"What's Pittsburgh like?" Jim asked Ikey as they grazed their horses by the towpath.

"Oh, it's a hundred times bigger than Cleveland," Ikey replied, more talkative than usual.

"Yeh?" Jim said, encouraging Ikey to continue, but they heard the distinctive sound of their own boat horn, calling the crew back.

"You'll see," Ikey smiled mysteriously.

"Let's go 'round together," Jim suggested.

"Not with me," Ikey replied as he turned to leave.

As the steamboat pulled the *Evening Star* and ten other canalboats into the Ohio River, Jim saw an endless expanse of water, so wide that the Cuyahoga seemed the size of the creek that ran past their cabin. And yet, the great waterway was partially hidden by the numerous boats that navigated it.

The *Evening Star* passed flatboats headed downstream—some twenty feet long but others over a hundred. Their decks were loaded with horses, cattle, tobacco, or grain.

Keelboats floated upriver—narrow crafts, almost as long as canalboats but only drawing a few inches of water. Their crews walked back and forth on long boards that flanked each side, forcing their long setting poles against the river bottom to push their boats upstream.

As the *Evening Star* rounded the last bend in the Ohio, Jim saw his first river steamboat—a travelers' palace. Two or three decks rose above the bottom one, which was only a few feet above the water line. The side paddlewheels sprayed a veil of water that enhanced the boat's wedding cake appearance.

Someday I'm gonna ride all the way to New Orleans on a steamboat like that, Jim promised himself.

The Ohio ended here in a wide basin that became two rivers—the Allegheny and the Monongahela. A point of land now called Pittsburgh split the river. The town was crowded close to the water's edge by the mountains behind it. At first all Jim could see were smokestacks trailing a gray mist through the sky. Then as the steamer pulled the *Evening Star* into the Monongahela, Jim could see buildings strung along the river's edge. Duplicates of the boats he had already seen were tied up along each side. Before reaching the huge bridge that connected the triangle to the opposite shore, the *Evening Star* cut loose from the tugboat. Now the crew poled it slowly into a wharf at the foot of Short Street to wait for shipping to resume on Monday.

Jim had completed his first canal trip on August 26, 1848. Quickly the crew left the boat to spend a Saturday night in Pittsburgh, except for Captain Letcher, who had to guard the cargo.

In the hours before darkness, Jim walked up Penn Street and down Liberty, along Redoubt

Alley and Garrison Way. He saw steam engine and glass factories and breweries that oozed a moldering stench. Raw iron, coal, corn, and cotton came into the city on boats and wagons; glass, cloth, whiskey, copper kettles, and iron wheels moved out the same way.

Pittsburgh was a city of merchants, doctors, lawyers, artisans, and laborers, who brought with them the New England belief that work was all-important. And so Pittsburgh grew to be the most important city west of the Appalachian Mountains.

But the city had another population. They were the drifters—wagoners, rivermen, free Negroes, and canallers like himself. They spent lonely, dangerous days on the trails and rivers. On Saturday nights, they turned to drinking, which led to stealing, fighting, and vandalism. Jim learned to stay away from dark alleys and to look over his shoulder, for he had no companion to rescue him.

Finally he wandered away from the noisy streets to Grant's Hill. Too excited to sleep, he watched this strange city from above.

Imagine a city with street lights and water that comes out of pipes inside your house! Jim thought. He fell asleep wondering at the lighted outline that lay below him.

On Sunday morning the respectable citizens of Pittsburgh took over again. Soon Jim heard the chiming of church bells—he counted fifty steeples as the sun broke over their peaks.

When he noticed a few people moving on the streets below, he decided it was time to return to the city. Jim wanted to see the old blockhouses of Fort Pitt, formerly Fort Duquesne. George Washington and General Braddock had fought against the French and Indians here long before Moses Cleaveland ever saw the entrance to the Cuyahoga River.

As he walked through the dusty streets in the heart of the city, Jim saw the shells of buildings consumed by the great fire of three years before. But even a disastrous fire had not stopped Pittsburgh; rebuilding was everywhere. *If I ever decide to leave the canal, I could sure find a job as a carpenter here,* he thought.

As he passed through the diamond that was the public square, he was stopped by the powerful voice of a man standing above a crowd of men.

"And I say to you, chase the Catholics out! They and their red cardinal are building the biggest church in all Pittsburgh. They say it's a cathedral. Next thing the pope himself will be here, condemning us all to hell."

The intensity of the man's words made Jim stop and listen further. Others seemed caught, too—frontiersmen, railroaders, steamboaters. Jim nudged a man standing next to him. "Who's he?"

"That's Preacher Joe Barker," he answered, annoyed that anyone would have to ask.

"Throw them out—those bead-fingering micks. Us Scots threw them out three hundred years ago—and their Queen Mary with them. Chopped her head off, we did. Our ancestors came here to get away from them, and now they're here. They'll take over, just like they did in Europe. Do you want that?"

"No!" shouted the crowd.

"Then we must drive them out. Burn their houses and churches. They have no place in Pittsburgh, or America!" His voice rose to accent his plea.

Quickly, Jim moved away. He had never heard a preacher talk about hating other Christians. Of course, most people back home were Baptists, Methodists, and Congregationalists. But from what he had read, Jim knew Americans were allowed to worship as they wished. Joe Barker's words and the crowd's rousing agreement angered him.

Closer to the fort, Jim heard another street corner preacher, one obviously hired by the good citizens of Pittsburgh to bring God's word to poor transients like himself.

This preacher seemed to be talking to Jim. How did he know Jim had stopped to watch a prize fight the night before? Had he seen Jim look at the fancy women or glance into saloon windows? He hadn't gone in. Nor had he gambled in the street corner games. His calloused hands had reminded him that he had worked hard for the little money he had.

Then why did the preacher's words seem to apply to him? Was he saying that someday Jim might look like the tough-faced men standing nearby? That leaving home to become a sailor meant he would end up like this?

No, Jim argued with himself. *Oliver Perry was a fine man, and so was John Paul Jones. Of course . . . they weren't canallers,* he remembered.

9

NO COWARDS NAMED GARFIELD

ON MONDAY, AUGUST 28, a steamer towed the *Evening Star* up the Monongahela River to a copper mill, where the crew unloaded the ore. Jim had seen mills in Cleveland, but none as big as the ones in Pittsburgh. Americans did not have to import iron kettles from England any longer. They could get all they needed right here—and cheaply. Canalboats headed downstream piled high with iron kettles for Wisconsin and Michigan. But the biggest products of these mills were iron rails. Trains did not come to Cleveland yet. But more than one railroad chugged into Pittsburgh. Their long whistles sounded far louder than the bowman's horn.

After the canalboat was unloaded, a steamer towed it back down the Monongahela to Pittsburgh and the Ohio River. The Ohio's downstream current was swift, so the *Evening*

Star quickly reached the canal basin at Beaver and returned to the canal. Jim hitched up Kit and Nance and was soon back on the towpath, pulling the *Star* up the Pennsylvania Canal toward Youngstown. At Youngstown, the boat's hold was loaded with sixty tons of coal to take to Cleveland.

But there was no time off when the *Evening Star* returned to Cleveland. They unloaded coal one day and took on lumber and barrels of salt the next. On September 4, they headed back toward Akron. Only this trip Jim did not walk the towpath.

The bowman had quit when they docked in Cleveland, giving Captain Letcher no time to search for another one. Although Jim had fallen into the canal fourteen times on the trip to Pittsburgh, the captain had been impressed by how quickly he had learned his own job, and others, too. Letcher made Jim bowman at the sumptuous salary of fourteen dollars a month. Now Jim only walked the towpath when he had to go ahead to make sure the water in the lock was down. If not, he ordered the lockkeeper to lower it. Then he returned to the bow and waited for the right moment to throw a bowline around the snubbing post and ease the *Evening Star* into the lock.

He had other duties, too: he worked on the deck securing cargo, filled the running lights and lanterns with oil, and trimmed their wicks. And he warned the crew, "Low bridge, everybody down!" when the *Evening Star* approached the low-lying bridges canallers cursed. Everybody had to stoop down or drop flat on the deck to keep from being knocked into the water.

But the aqueducts were even worse. The first one Jim had encountered was between Cleveland and Akron at Brecksville. Here the canal came to the Cuyahoga River, whose sides were too steep and narrow at this point to build locks. So the builders erected a bridge across the Cuyahoga and filled it with water so the canalboat could float across.

The crew tensed each time they approached an aqueduct, particularly the one close to Akron at Peninsula. It was built of quarried stone with a few narrow boards that served as a towpath. Here the hoggee always tightened his hold on the horses—one misstep and the team would fall in. Dave held the sweep steady—any abrupt variation would send the canalboat grinding into the side of the aqueduct, jamming the boat crosswise. Because only one boat could go through an aqueduct at a time, a jammed boat would halt canal traffic for hours or days, until the boat was freed.

Now that it was September—the driest season of the year—the crew also had to watch or the *Evening Star* would stick fast on the mud and debris along the sides of the canal. The water level was dropping even in sections with a good supply from the feeder lakes and rivers.

One day the boat stuck especially fast. Captain

Every man strained against the iron-tipped poles.

Letcher ordered the whole crew to man the setting poles.

Every man strained against the long, iron-tipped poles. Suddenly the *Evening Star* broke loose. The quick jerk wrenched Jim's pole out of his hands and knocked Dave to the deck.

"I'm sorry," Jim apologized. "When the boat broke loose, I couldn't hold my pole. Are you hurt?" Jim extended his hand to help Dave to his feet.

But all the contempt Dave had felt for Jim reinforced his anger at being knocked down. He turned his fall into a crouch and sprang up, running toward Jim, swearing like that captain in Cleveland Harbor.

Jim stopped apologizing and prepared to fight. The swearing no longer shocked him. He waited calmly, determined to beat this man who had tormented him since his first night on the canal. Just as Dave was about to reach him, Jim jumped out of the way and hit him hard on the jaw. Dave fell among the barrels of salt in the bottom of the boat.

All the crew watched this battle between the toughest fighter on the canal and the cowardly farm boy, while the *Evening Star* drifted rudderless in mid-canal.

"Pound the fool to death!" Captain Letcher urged Jim, but he did not try to protect his cousin. This was a matter between two canallers.

Not willing to lose his advantage, Jim jumped on Dave as he lay stunned. Now he could beat him senseless. Jim started to raise his fist, knowing Dave was ready for whatever Jim wanted to give him. Dave asked no quarter nor did his eyes beg for mercy.

I can't, Jim thought. *This man's down. It would be wrong to hit him just 'cause I can.* Jim lowered his fist and let Dave up.

Grudgingly, the middle-aged man apologized to the boy and limped off. Jim rubbed the knuckles of his right hand as Cook, Ikey, and the other crewmen came up and slapped him on the back.

"Makes you the toughest man on the canawl," Ikey said. "Wait'll I tell the boys my old stablemate made Dave crawl."

"Yeh," laughed Cook. "I didn't know Dave knew how to apologize. All I ever heard outta him were the wrong words." The whole crew laughed.

"Get this boat under control!" Captain Letcher ordered. He manned the sweep himself. The rest of them grabbed the setting poles to return the *Evening Star* to the center of the canal.

"Ready, you hoggee?" Letcher yelled to the new driver.

When the *Evening Star* was under way again, Letcher leaned back and smiled. "My ma always said there weren't no cowards named Garfield," he muttered to the canal.

10

MUDLARKED!

ON JIM'S FIRST TRIP as bowman, the *Evening Star* stayed on the Ohio and Erie Canal instead of taking the Crosscut to Pittsburgh. Now the canal was a fifty-to-sixty-foot ribbon through an enveloping wilderness. All traces of where crews of twenty, thirty, or fifty men had worked fifteen years before, building the bank up on one side and flattening a generous towpath on the other, were gone. Nature closed in, trying to reclaim its own.

Jim felt at ease in this environment, for life here was like that in Orange. The canalboat glided past isolated farms, and men, women, and children waved hello to the welcome intruders.

The patches of civilization at towns like Clinton, Canal Fulton, Bolivar, and Dover were expanding. A few clapboard and brick houses were beginning to replace some of the log cabins. Here the canals were wider, but passage was still difficult. Freight boats tied up anywhere to deliver their cargoes. Barrels, casks, kegs, and bales were strewn along the bank with little organization. When the *Star* delivered barrels of salt or lengths of lumber, the crew used their setting poles to shove into a bank crowded by many other boats. Often the other crews pushed back, so a duel with setting poles was not uncommon.

Even passenger travel suffered in these outpost towns. People often boarded a packet boat by jumping onto the boat's roof from the top of a lock or low bridge. And once they were on, passengers had to keep their balance or get wet in the canal—there were no protective railings. Even freight boats only had a toe rail a few inches high to keep the cargo from sliding off. When the *Evening Star* caught on a snag or bounced off the bank, Jim came close to falling overboard if he was near the edge of the deck.

But he was determined not to fall in the canal again. He was a bowman now, and the crew was spreading Dave's defeat as fast as their boat traveled. Now the crew accepted him as a useful member and forgot his clumsiness and supposed cowardice. He was part of the one-for-all-and-all-for-one security on each boat.

One day as the boat approached Port Washington, Dave suddenly yelled to Jim, "Bowman, sound your horn to drop the line. Hurry-up boat apassin'!"

Jim almost lost his balance as Dave turned the *Evening Star* sharply into the berm bank. Quickly Jim sounded the signal to tell Ikey to drop his towrope. Then Jim heard the unusual sound of pounding hooves, indicating a speed well over the four-mile-per-hour limit. Any captain that tried to push his team to six or seven miles paid a heavy fine to the pathmasters, hired by the canal company as patrols. Excessive speeds ruined the canal, churning up the water and washing away the banks.

Within moments a long, narrow boat, unlike any other, sped by him, leaving a crashing wake in the shallow water.

Captain Letcher was swearing and stamping on the deck.

"What was that?" Jim asked.

"Trouble!" Letcher snapped.

"Whadda you wanna do, cap'n?" asked Dave. "Pull ahead or wait here?"

"Pull ahead. Might as well get in line," Letcher answered. "Sound your horn, Jim. Pull, you hoggee!" he ordered Ikey up the path.

Captain Letcher continued to mumble angrily. Within a mile Ikey stopped the team, and the towrope fell slack. "Dam ahead!" Ikey called back.

Jim could see many boats tied to both sides of the canal.

"Jim! Put lines to the trees fore and aft," barked the captain.

"Ikey! Bring the team on board." Letcher threw the towrope off the deadeye himself. "Get out shovels and let's go!" he ordered. "Cook, stay aboard. Have food ready at sundown!"

The crew followed their captain up the towpath.

"What's goin' on?" Jim whispered to Ikey. "What boat went by so fast?"

"Must be a big leak in the canal ahead," Ikey explained. "The hurry-up boat and all the men in it were rushin' to get there."

"What are we suppose to do with these shovels?" asked Jim as they joined crews from other canal-boats carrying their shovels.

"We're gonna dig all day and all night!" Ikey spat on the ground in disgust.

As they arrived at the leak, a big man Jim had seen on the hurry-up boat gave orders to the various crews. "Letcher, put your men to work fellin' trees for the north dam."

"Ain't got no axes, only shovels," answered the captain.

"Get axes out of the repair boat!" he ordered.

Within an hour, farmers and their wives and children appeared with horses and wagons. Their horses pulled the fallen trees to the canal and the men from the hurry-up boat maneuvered the timbers into place to slow the water. "Men!—into the canal!" ordered the pathmaster.

There was still water in the canal and mud below that. Standing up to his knees in water, Jim began digging into the canal bottom. But the wet mud he threw against the timbers just slid off. Other men threw straw down. Mixed with straw, the mud began to stick. Two dams—twenty-six feet wide at the bottom and forty feet wide at the top—had to be built.

When the crew went back to the *Evening Star* for supper, the boat was mudlarked on the dry bottom of the canal. After a quick meal, they returned to the leak. Now the towpath was crowded with farmers' wagons traveling back and forth between sections that still had enough water to float the boats. They carried passengers and perishable goods around the break, so they could continue their journey.

All night a hundred men—and even women—dug, threw, and pounded dirt into the break in the canal wall. Lanterns and bull's-eyes from the boats were hung everywhere for light.

By the time dawn broke, Jim and Ikey were so exhausted they could not lift their shovels. They watched anxiously as the pathmaster walked back and forth, swinging his lantern to study the repair. Would it hold?

As the tired men waited, he finally pronounced it sound.

"Tear down the dams!" he ordered.

"Now?" protested Jim. "We gotta get some rest first."

"We gotta open the canawl first!" said some

muddy man standing nearby. "Cain't make no money with mudlarked boats on a dammed-up canal."

Jim groaned as he dug his shovel into the north dam he had spent all yesterday building.

It was midnight before Jim felt the *Star's* slight motion as it began to float again. The canal had begun to fill with water from the feeder lakes. But Jim hoped the captain would not notice for a while, so they could rest a little longer.

Jim slapped at the mosquitoes and kicked a mouse that scampered over his feet. "You dumb critter. Nothin' to eat here." He went back to sleep.

But there was never much sleep on a canalboat, just snatches. The boat had to keep moving. Night or day, cold or hot, wet or dry, a hoggee had to be out on the towpath, a steersman had to man the sweep, and a bowman had to be ready to lock through.

At night, Jim hung a bull's-eye lantern on the bow lighting up the canal and towpath for almost two hundred feet ahead.

But in the fog and rain, the light did not penetrate far. As the rain poured down one night, Jim kept adjusting the wick and the reflector to get more light out of the bull's eye as he strained to see the lanterns hung on the next lock. Jim knew Ikey must be having a hard time driving the horses without the added light. Except for Dave at the tiller, the rest of the crew was sleeping. The three of them were responsible for the boat's safe journey.

Jim stepped on the tow rail and leaned forward to see if the lantern was giving any more light. The rail was wet, and Jim felt clumsy in his heavy oil cloth coat. Suddenly the boat lurched off the bank. Jim lost his balance and pitched into the dark water in front of the boat.

In an instant, the *Evening Star* was above him, its hull within inches of his head. He fought to push himself out from under the boat and surface for air. Then he felt a rope dragging in the water.

Saved! he thought. But the rope uncoiled limply in his hand. It had not been made fast.

"Help!" he screamed as he began to sink again.

But the muddy water gagged him, and he could not be heard. Neither Ikey far ahead on the towpath nor Dave at the sweep could tell he was not in the bow. He was alone. He clutched the useless rope as he struggled to get his head above water. But the heavy coat weighed him down, and the weeds entangled his feet. If only he knew how to swim. The bank was only ten feet away!

Suddenly, he felt the rope go tight. Jim's hands gripped it like a vice, and soon his head broke the top of the water. Coughing and choking to get air, he let himself be dragged along behind the boat. Finally he realized the rope could go. *I've got to get hold of the boat!* he thought. Somehow, he lifted his heavy arms and pulled himself to the boat as it headed downstream.

"Dave! Help me!" he called weakly. But the rain muffled his words.

Holding onto the gunnel with one hand, he managed to force the bulky coat off. Then he slowly hoisted himself up and over the side to the *Star's* deck. As he lay there, he noticed that the knotted end of the rope had caught in a crack at the very edge of the deck. That crack had saved his life!

He shook as he thanked God for his deliverance. That crack seemed more than the caprice of fate. His mother had said she would pray for him. Now he knew God had heard her. *I ain't even sent her a message that I'm all right, yet she's kept on praying for me,* he told himself. *I know she has.*

In that moment Jim remembered all his mother had said. She hadn't wanted him to become a sailor. She had wanted him to get more schooling and become a teacher. Maybe God wanted him to be something better than a canaller, too.

But before Jim could think further, the lights of the next lock appeared in the rain like yellow ghosts. He struggled up to find his bowline and get ready to lock through.

By the next day, Jim forgot his doubts. He stood at the bow, confidently guiding the *Evening Star* into another lock. He was a good bowman—Captain Letcher's approving glances told him that. Someday he would captain a ship bound for China, just as he had dreamed.

11

AGUE

JIM WAS BACK on the towpath. Ikey had fallen ill with fever two days before and lay in the cook's shack. The *Evening Star* had to keep moving, which meant two hoggees alternating their teams.

Only a few days before, Captain Letcher had told the crew he hoped to get in an extra trip or two before the canals froze over. If the good weather held, they could all expect the added pay. Now with Ikey sick and the crew splitting the extra work, Letcher only hoped they would make it back to Cleveland.

The towpath was now a net of mosquitoes. The rains, without a frost, caused them to swarm up from the green muck along the canal and out of the dense woods that lined the towpath like a wall. So Jim carried thick branches. He waved a short one over himself; the long one he waved over the tortured Kit and Nance.

Ikey was not the only one sick. In the towns along the canals, many people were ill with the ague. Some staggered weakly around in the morning, only to be struck down in the afternoon by a bout of chills, aching, and fever. The farmers began to grumble that the sickness was caused by the canals. And old-timers remembered how the great plague of cholera in 1832 had moved along the canals and rivers from Montreal to New Orleans, killing thousands as it went. More than a few said the canals should be done away with.

But all Jim worried about was how the shorthanded crew would ever pole the *Evening Star* down the Portage Summit Cascade. When they were locking through No. 5 on the way down the Cascade, Captain Letcher yelled at Jim: "Tighten up on that rope! You're lettin' the *Star* go into the wall!"

Jim pulled with all his might, but that was not enough. His head had ached for hours, and he longed for a drink. Hearing the rush of water as it drained out of the locks made him more thirsty. Jim pulled harder, keeping the boat steady as the lock drained. But on the Cascade, the *Evening Star* moved out of one lock and immediately into another. Again and again he had to push the setting pole and strain to keep the rope tight.

After Lock No. 21, the towpath began again. Jim

hitched a team to one end of the towrope. Captain Letcher fastened the other end to the dead-eye. When Ikey heard these familiar sounds, he staggered out of the cook's shack.

"I been restin' long enough," he said. "I can drive my shift." But then suddenly he sat down on a keg.

Jim wished Ikey could drive, because his own head pounded and his legs felt like pudding.

"Naw, you still look a mite shaky. Best you rest a spell longer," Jim said unconvincingly.

Captain Letcher joined them, and after seeing Ikey's flushed face, told him to lie down again.

"But cap'n, I can do my job," Ikey insisted, fearful the captain might put him off and withhold his season's wages.

"That's an order!" Captain Letcher said sternly. "Jim'll drive."

Jim said nothing as he prepared to take the horses across the gangplank. He would try to make it to Cleveland for his cousin's sake.

The canal ran along for a mile to Lock No. 23, where the Little Cuyahoga joined the main Cuyahoga River. Then there were three locks together. After Lock No. 26, called Mud Catcher, the canal was flat until Pan Cake. But at Peninsula, Jim had to maneuver the horses along the few narrow boards that served as a towpath for the aqueduct. One waver in his steady grip and the horses could stumble into the canal. Somehow Jim held on, even through the next series of locks, which were extremely close together. He wanted to climb on Kit's back and ride for a while, but not until he was through Lock No. 36 at Brecksville, which was the hardest because it joined two aqueducts.

After that the locks were farther apart, and Jim did ride for a while. But by the time the *Evening Star* let down in Lock No. 42 at the foot of Superior Street to float onto the Cuyahoga River, Jim lay in the cook's shack next to Ikey.

Captain Letcher secured the canalboat near the iron mill that was to receive the coal and set the remaining crew to work unloading. Then he went in to see Jim and Ikey.

"Jim, I'm gonna find a farmer goin' toward Orange. He can take you home," he explained.

Jim protested. "I'll be fine in a day or two. I can't leave the canal. Ain't the end of the season yet and where will you find another bowman and hoggee?" Jim lay back, exhausted by his speech.

"You ever had the ague before?" Letcher asked.

"I had fever before," Jim grumbled.

"But not this kind. This is a bad one, Jim. You need care like only your own ma can give you. It's already October 3rd, and we'll probably be closin' down soon with so much sickness."

"Can I come back when I'm well, captain?" Jim asked cautiously.

"Proud to have a tough canaller like you in my crew," he answered.

Jim closed his eyes. He hated to go home after only seven weeks as a canaller. But maybe it was God's will that he return for a while. Maybe mother or Tom needed him.

"Letcher! Amos Letcher! Where you be?" shouted a familiar voice.

Letcher looked toward the bow to see his uncle, Thomas Garfield, standing in the middle of the deck, his foot on the deadeye, bellowing for him.

"Uncle Thomas! Here! What brings you to the docks?" Amos Letcher greeted him. "Nothin' happened to my ma or pa?"

Thomas laughed. "No, Amos. Nothin's happened to your folks. 'Tis business that brings me not misfortune."

Amos relaxed.

"I got lumber to go up the canal to Cochocton. Can you take it for me? Or are you contracted for?"

Amos Letcher scratched his head. "Well, I got problems, uncle, and I'm glad you're here. Uncle Abram's boy Jim been workin' for me for the last couple months."

"Jim's been workin' on the canal?" Thomas Garfield interrupted. "That young scalawag. His ma's been worried sick, wonderin' what's happened to him. He left home right after he finished a job for me, and nobody's heard of him since. I know his ma's been prayin' for him night and day."

"Well, Jim's here, uncle," Amos Letcher continued. "But he's down with the ague. He'd best get home, so his ma can take care of him. My other hoggee's down, too. Soon as either my brothers come with supplies, I'm sendin' him to our place at Bryan. He ain't got no folks."

"Well, I got my wagon. I can take Jim back to Newburgh with me, then me or Charles can get him to Orange."

"Thanks," the captain said, sounding relieved. "I was just goin' to look for a wagon goin' that way, or take him myself if I hadda. Feel much better if kinfolk are lookin' out for him." Amos paused to change the subject. "Now, about your lumber. If I can hire another hoggee and a bowman, I can make at least one more trip before the freeze. When my brothers come, maybe I can use 'em if the harvest is in at home. But it might take me a couple of days," Amos warned.

"Send word to me at Newburgh," Thomas replied. "Now I better get Charles to help me with Jim."

The sun had been down three hours when Charles Garfield drove slowly down the rutted road in front of the log cabin three miles from Orange.

"Here you be," Jim's cousin said to notify him they were finally home.

Jim, who had been holding his aching head, looked up. He could just make out the outlines of the cabin against the dark forest. A dim light shone from the two front windows, and smoke curled out of the chimney. Jim was chilled by the cool October night, despite the blanket his Uncle Thomas had wrapped around him.

"Put your horse in the barn over there, Charles. Mother can get us somethin' to eat."

"No, thank you, Jim. I'll go on to Uncle Amos Boynton's tonight. It's just a little up the road," he answered. "Your ma's gonna have enough to do takin' care of you."

Jim was too sick to argue. He started to climb down awkwardly from the front seat of the wagon. Charles offered to help him, but Jim would not allow it, and Charles understood.

"Thank you, Charles. Mighty kind of Uncle Thomas to spare you. I coulda walked," Jim said, still refusing to admit how sick he was.

"Hadda come this way anyway to pick up some wood from Uncle Amos. Wasn't outta my way a bit," Charles lied. "Goodnight, Jim. Take care of yourself and stop by Newburgh on your way back to the canal." Charles slapped the reins, and the wagon moved away.

Jim slowly dragged his aching body toward the door.

For ten days Jim lay in his mother's bed in the corner of the cabin. She sat beside him night and day as the fever drove the sense out of him. There was no ice, so Tom drew cool buckets of water from the creek to moisten the cloth on Jim's forehead. His mother changed the compress every few minutes and sponged his arms and legs with the cool water. But it helped little.

Once Jim opened his delirious eyes and looked up at the dill, mustard, and basil drying from the rafters in bunches. As they swayed in the breeze, Jim screamed, thinking they were trees falling on him.

The sight of hams and bacon hung up to cure was even worse. Their smell added to the nausea of his sickness and made him retch until his mother had Tom remove them from the cabin. He was thirsty, constantly thirsty. His mother supported his head as he drank sips from cup after cup of water, only to release the moisture from his sweating pores.

Constantly, he was surrounded by the murmur of his mother's prayers. She thanked God for bringing her son back instead of letting him die among strangers. She prayed he might not be taken from her again, by death.

Eliza Garfield had nursed many others through the ague. And she had suffered this dread sickness more than once. Finally, her prayers were answered. By the end of October, the fever broke, and Jim improved.

Yet the strong muscles that had chopped 100 cords of wood a few months earlier had been weakened. Eliza kept the fire roaring under her cooking irons as she fed Jim broth, puddings, and stews to make him strong again.

But when a little strength returned, he stood shakily on his feet and rewarded her by announcing, "I'm goin' back to the canal."

Mrs. Garfield said nothing. She did not say that if he had listened to her, he would not be suffering so. Nor did she remind him that years before, the canal had cost her and her husband everything they had, including their health. She merely replied, "James, we'll trust God to show us the way."

But if it was God's way, it seemed strange that Jim fell ill again by the second week in November. He would wake up in the morning free of fever, able to get around and eat his breakfast and noon dinner. Then the shaking would begin. He would stand close to the fire, and his mother would bring him a quilt. But as the fever returned, he would collapse onto the bed and pile more quilts on, only to push them off again as he burned with fever. His head ached so he hardly wanted to live.

By early evening, the fever and chills would leave, and by morning, the headache was gone, too. But each morning he was weaker than the one before. Soon Eliza Garfield sent for Doctor Butler.

Butler had been doctoring on the frontier for many years. Like the great majority of men who called themselves doctors, he had never attended a college of medicine. Although he knew that bleeding a patient was not good, he relied on ground herbs, barks, and berries to help the sick. Jim's mother would have done just as well to call in the old granny woman folks secretly believed to be a good witch. She would have told Jim to wear a live spider around his neck and drink his own urine. Or Eliza Garfield could have called in the Indian medicine man, who would have made a strong drink from sassafras roots. Some people thought grannies and medicine men knew more about curing folks than doctors.

But they all relied on plants to help their patients. If the patient was cured, the same potions were tried on the next sick person.

November became December. Then it was January, 1849, and Doctor Butler's pills had not helped Jim. Now he did not even feel well in the mornings.

Soon after the New Year, they were surprised by an unexpected knock on the door. Tom was tending the stock, so Eliza went to answer.

"Good day, Aunt Eliza," Captain Letcher said.

"Amos!" Eliza replied, her mouth set grimly.

"Come to see how Jim is and to pay him his wages." Captain Letcher hoped his explanation would soften Eliza's cold greeting.

Mrs. Garfield reluctantly invited him to step in.

Hearing the captain's voice, Jim struggled to sit up. "Cap'n Letcher!" he called in a voice surprisingly strong.

Amos Letcher was shocked to see his former employee's condition, but he tried to sound cheerful. "Well, Jim, are you still restin' up? I brought your wages. I know I been delayed, but we worked the canal way into November."

Jim was so glad to see the captain he smiled and began asking questions. "How many more trips did you get? Did you go by way of the Crosscut?"

"Well, we went to Cochocton. Took us pretty near two weeks, because then we went to Portsmouth on the Ohio. Didn't have to go to Pittsburgh again."

"How's Ikey? Did he get better?"

"Well, Ikey's over the ague, but he don't have much strength back yet," the captain answered.

Jim fell back exhausted, even though he had much more he wanted to ask.

Amos Letcher could see this, and he could not help frowning as he pulled some bills from his pocket and counted out Jim's wages.

But Jim shook his head. "Give it to mother. She'll know what to do with it."

Amos nodded.

"Cap'n?" Jim struggled up on one elbow. "When are you puttin' the *Evening Star* back on the canal?"

"Well, don't rightly know, Jim. Depends on when the spring thaw comes. Sometimes it can fool you. Gets real warm in March, and then comes a blizzard in April and your boat freezes in the canal.

Depends too on when the canawl companies get around to bottoming out the ditch. Won't be for three, four months yet," Letcher said.

"Can I come back to the *Evening Star?* Or did you find another bowman?"

"Get your strength back, Jim, and then come and see me."

Eliza, standing by the fireplace, turned away, a look of pain on her face.

"Oh, I'll be fine by March or April," Jim assured him.

"I know you will. You're lookin' pretty fit now," the captain lied.

"Amos, let me give you some coffee and bread," Jim's mother offered, knowing how cold it was outside. "I want to hear about Sister Polly and your brothers and sister."

When Amos was seated at the table, he motioned for Eliza to take a bench, too. In a low voice he asked, "He been sick like this since he come home?"

Eliza nodded her head, her face still grim.

"You hadda doctor?" he asked.

"Doctor Butler from Orange," she replied. "But James ain't improving. He's so weak." Tears were in her eyes as she looked away.

"I don't know Butler, but call in a Doctor Harmon from over to Chagrin Falls. He got me on my feet after a bout of the ague a couple of years ago. Ain't never come back neither."

"Doctor Harmon? I will, Amos. I'll send Tom this very day." Eliza looked hopeful for the first time in weeks. "I'll be so thankful if only he gets well. Guess I won't even mind if he goes back to the canal," she added.

Still speaking in a low voice, the captain replied, "Your boy don't belong on the canawl."

Eliza Garfield stared at him.

"He's strong and works hard and don't complain, but he's too smart for the canawl. When I taught school out in Indiana for three winters, I seen two kinds of boys—smart ones and dumb ones. Jim's smart. Sometimes when we was goin' along peaceful on the canawl, he and I got to talkin'. He sure has read a lotta books. He needs more learnin'. Farmin' ain't for him neither. He'll just run away to sea again. Get him back to school if you can."

Eliza Garfield could think of nothing to reply, but tears returned to her eyes.

12

THE LONG WINTER

BY NIGHTFALL, Tom had fetched Doctor Harmon and a young man who was studying under him, Mr. H. Vincent. They examined Jim and listened carefully as Mrs. Garfield told them the history of his illness. They nodded; then Doctor Harmon spoke.

"If we were in New Orleans, we could get a medicine they use down there. It comes from the bark of a tree in South America, and it's called quinine. Sure cures bad cases of ague. But there isn't any here, so we'll have to use calomel. It's all we have."

Eliza Garfield winced. She had been dosed with calomel and knew how sick it made a person even as it cured him.

Doctor Harmon and his assistant measured out a large amount of the heavy white powder and mixed it in a mug of water for Jim to drink. Then they left Jim to the care of his mother and brother.

Soon Jim was bent double with cramps in his stomach, his knees drawn almost up to his chin. The pain was so bad it made him sweat even more. Eliza and Tom held him so he would not throw himself onto the floor. The cramping continued all night and most of the next day. Yet the doctors came again and repeated this dosage. Eliza Garfield prayed that the doctors would help Jim and not let him die like his father had. She tried not to curse the canal, but it had cost her so much. She had thought she was done with it twenty years ago. Now her son might die of the sickness some called canal fever.

Jim could not even lift his head to drink. His mother was not strong enough to care for him alone, so Tom left his work and stayed with them. But the doctors returned every day to give Jim more doses of calomel until he would have no more. After the first week and a half of January, the chills and fever left completely.

In a few days, Jim was able to sit propped up in bed. But there was no way his legs would support him if he stood. Now that his brain no longer raged with delirium and yet his body remained weak, he was restless. Eliza knew she must find him some books. She had nursed him through so many long months of convalescence in his childhood she knew only books would help him. And she knew just where to get them.

Since November, a young man had been teaching at the little schoolhouse on their land. He was one of the few people outside the family and the Boynton cousins that Tom talked to without restraint. And the new schoolmaster liked Tom. He had tried to persuade him to attend the evening school he set up for adults. But Tom had refused, saying it was his brother, Jim, who was the book learner.

By the third week in January, Jim was well enough for Eliza to invite Sam Bates over to dinner. As he took off his heavy coat that evening, he pulled books out of its great pockets.

Jim sat in his mother's rocking chair by the fire. He could not stand and greet Sam as a man normally would. But within a short time, the two young men were talking easily.

"How are you doing with those books I sent over earlier, Jim?" Sam asked.

"Oh, I finished them. In fact, *Napoleon* was so interesting, I read it twice."

"I gave your mother all the reading books I had, so I brought over an arithmetic and speller this time. Your mother said you haven't been to school for almost a year."

"I guess it has been that long," Jim answered.

"Everybody needs as much schooling as he can get, no matter what kind of work he does," Sam asserted. "You do farming mostly?"

"I'm a canaller," snapped Jim. He was not sure if

seven weeks on the canal made him a professional, but he felt like a veteran. "As soon as I get my strength back, I'm goin' back to the canal for a while. Then I'm goin' to be a lake sailor."

Sam was a little taken back by Jim's sharp answer but he continued cheerfully. "You're a canaller? That must be interesting work. You must have been lots of places and met lots of different folks."

Soon Jim was telling Sam of his experiences, many of which his mother and Tom heard for the first time. Near the end of the supper of biscuits, boiled victuals, and applesauce, Jim became tired and thought to ask Sam about himself.

"Well, my folks live over near Marion. I grew up there. But the last four terms, I've been attending Geauga Academy over to Chester."

Eliza Garfield nodded her head approvingly. "Tell us about the academy, Sam. What do you study there?"

"All kinds of things—Greek, Latin, grammar, natural and moral science, algebra, philosophy." Sam spoke in snatches as he remembered the different subjects.

"They teach all that?" Jim asked unbelievingly. Geauga Academy seemed different from the log schoolhouse he had always attended.

"Why, sure," Sam replied. "We had eight teachers and over two hundred students this last year, about half boys and half girls."

Sam came to the Garfield cabin often. And since Jim was not strong enough to travel, his cousins and friends began to meet there, too. Because the fields were covered with snow and only light chores had to be done, these nights started early and ended late. Sometimes they met at others' homes, and the girls joined them for parties and singing. At these gatherings, Sam talked about Geauga Academy and began to urge some of them to attend the spring term, among them Jim's cousin William Boynton.

Each day Jim gained a little strength, but very little. Every morning he told himself he was going to be stronger. He would get out of bed before Tom or his mother were up, dressed, build up the fire, and went out to milk the cows. Then he ate a hardy breakfast and chopped some wood. But his arms would barely lift the axe, and he quickly broke into a sweat. He would have to rest. The plentiful noon meal renewed him, so he would attempt to repair the cabin roof or the side of the barn. By midafternoon, he was asleep in the loft. For the rest of the day and evening, he could only read and talk. Day after day he tried to be stronger—and he was. But not strong enough—not enough to throw his weight against a setting pole in the twenty-two locks of the Cascade or hold the rope around a snubbing post to keep the *Star* off the walls of the lock.

One evening Sam suggested he come over to the

school and refresh his memory.

"With all those kids?" Jim scoffed.

"What do you mean, kids? Your cousins and friends come," Sam answered. "You gonna sit around here forever? It's better than doing nothing."

Jim had not been in the schoolhouse since the last day of the term almost a year ago. Now as he slumped onto the back row of benches, it was all too familiar. He had attended this school since he was six or seven years old and sat on the front benches.

But during the year he had been gone, he had crossed the invisible line between boyhood and manhood. He had left his childhood. Jim went to day school a few times, but then he could go no longer. Sometimes he attended the evening school Sam taught occasionally.

One morning the last week in February, Jim was feeling stronger than usual. He turned to his mother and said, "I think I oughta let Amos Letcher know I wanna work on the *Evenin' Star* when the canal opens."

His mother replied calmly, "James, you're not fully recovered. I know the ague's course. If a body tires to do too much, he's struck down again."

Jim knew she spoke the truth. "But what am I gonna do? Help Tom on the farm this spring? My learnin' to be a sailor will get pushed back again."

"Why don't you go to school for a few months?"

"School's almost over for this year," he said irritably, as if his mother were stupid not to realize that. "Besides, I'm too big to go there."

"Not our school, James. I mean the academy where Sam Bates goes. It's only ten miles away in Chester."

Now Jim was really annoyed. He had been thinking of the school and the 150 books in its library. "We don't have the money, mother. You heard Sam tell what it costs." He paused to consider her suggestion and then decided out loud, "I need to work out—on the canal or someplace—and bring money in, not take it."

"James, listen to me. If you go to school this spring—and maybe next fall, you can teach in the winter like Sam Bates. After that, you can work the canal in the summer if you want to. That's what Amos Letcher did before he got his own boat," she added.

Jim was stopped by her idea. Captain Letcher had been a schoolteacher. Maybe that was why he was a captain and Dave only a steersman, even though Letcher was the younger man.

"But what about the money?" Jim reminded her.

"Tom and I got seventeen dollars saved up. You take it and go to school. You ain't good for nothin' sittin' around here," she said a little scornfully.

Jim was hurt. His mother had not talked to him like that since he came home. Now she was implying he was a shiftless dreamer.

"I'll think on it, mother" was all Jim would say.

"Pray on it, James. Maybe it's God's will you are not strong yet. Maybe he wants you to use your mind."

Jim had done nothing for five months. *What choice do I have?* he wondered. *I'll go for one term. By midsummer I'll return to sailin' and pay mother and Tom back.*

13

THE ACADEMY

ON MARCH 6, Jim, his look-alike cousin William Boynton, and their friend Orrin Judd walked the ten miles to Geauga Academy. If Jim had walked from Orange to Chester alone, he probably would not have made it. But Orrin's and William's enthusiasm made the ten-mile walk seem less strenuous. Each of them carried a load of supplies: bacon, ham, bread, and quilts, plus a little extra clothing.

In his pocket, Jim had the seventeen dollars his mother and Tom had insisted he take, although he had protested he could make do with less. He wished his canal wages had not gone to pay for medicine and the doctor bills. Jim had been so sure he could make his mother's life more comfortable by sending his sailor's pay home. Now here he was taking instead of giving.

When the boys finally reached the banks of the Chagrin River, they saw the large academy building sitting high on the bluff. The plain wooden building seemed impressive to boys who had attended tiny log cabin schools.

As they walked through Chester, they noticed a few houses with signs in the windows: Rooms for Scholars.

"Let's try this house. We need to rent a room before they're all gone," William suggested.

But Jim wanted to wait. "We'll go to the school and see if they have a list of places to stay at prices they consider fair."

"But, Jim, it's gettin' late, and I don't have no mind to sleep outside tonight—still too cold," William argued.

"Do you wanna get slickered?" Jim asked. "I suppose your pa filled your pockets with gold pieces?"

"No, Jim. None of us got much money," William admitted.

"So we gotta shop careful and make what we got last," Jim added.

By evening the three boys had hired a room with two beds and a stove from a Mrs. Reed, who agreed to cook their meals and do their washing. They were too tired to set up the stove in their room or buy wood, so they endured a cold room for the first night.

The next day, they signed up for their courses.

Jim, his look-alike cousin William Boynton, and their friend Orrin Judd walked the ten miles to Geauga Academy.

The variety of subjects seemed like a frontier wedding, where there was so much food Jim did not know what to select. But unlike a wedding, the courses each cost fifty cents or one or two dollars. Jim looked over the list: algebra, philosophy, grammar, mental arithmetic, botany, geography, elocution, Latin, and Greek. He wanted to take them all in the one term he planned to be here, but he had to save some money for books and food. He settled on algebra, philosophy, and grammar. Singing school was free.

The next day, Jim sat on the first row of benches in the classroom, his hands clasped around one knee. He listened to every word the professor said, for he intended to get his money's worth.

As he was leaving the building after class, he heard a slightly familiar voice.

"That's Jim what's-his-name. What's the likes of him doin' here at the academy?"

Jim turned around to see Sarah Caldwell talking to a group of students and pointing at him. Some of the girls were snickering at his homespun shirt, patched pants, and old dusty boots.

If Jim had learned one thing since he had last seen Sarah, it was that no one could be judged by what appeared to the eye. And those who judged that way were not worth knowing. He pulled off his ragged straw hat and swept the group a sarcastic bow.

"Well, if it ain't Sarah, the salter's daughter,

from back home in Orange." Jim deliberately emphasized her first name. "Don't bother to introduce me to your friends; I don't wanna know them."

Then he popped his hat back on his head and sauntered away, stealing a look over his shoulder to see Sarah's reaction. He was pleased that she was marching away angrily in the other direction. But one girl whom he already knew, Lucretia Rudolph, turned and gave him a shy smile.

Despite Sarah and her few silly friends, Jim did not endure the ostracism here he had known on the canal. In less than a week, he joined the Zetelethian Debating Society and soon made many friends. Debates brought news and entertainment to people on the frontier, who seldom saw a newspaper. Anybody and everybody who could, debated. By the second meeting, the society had so many members, it split into two. Jim went with the new one, which loftily called itself the Sophomethians, or "Disciples of Wisdom."

Since joining societies was free, he also joined the phonography society, which studied a method devised by a Mr. Pittman to substitute marks for words and speed up writing. Soon Jim began taking his class notes in this shortened form.

Jim was up at five in the morning for classes and often did not finish studying or debate society meetings—of which he soon belonged to two—until eleven at night. Despite these long hours, he found himself enjoying school and wanted to share his experiences with his mother and Tom. The second weekend, he borrowed Mrs. Reed's horse and buggy and went home to Orange.

Jim drove slowly and carefully, for he did not want to knock off a wheel on the rough roads. But as he neared the cabin, he increased the horse's pace so he could drive up to the door with a dash.

"Oh, you haven't given up school already," Eliza Garfield said as she saw who their Saturday afternoon visitor was.

"No, mother. And I haven't been sent home for bein' a dunce either!"

Mrs. Garfield was pleased to see her son healthy enough to be joking. "Are you feelin' as good as you look?" she asked him.

"Yes, mother. I had no problem walking to Chester, and I've chopped some wood for our landlady, Mrs. Reed. It's part of our contract for boardin'."

Even though Jim now lived with a cousin who was almost like a brother, he was glad to be back in the cabin for a night with his mother and Tom. When the door was shut and barred and the latchstring pulled in, Jim stirred up the fire. His mother took her Bible down and read the same passages she had read every night that Jim could remember.

When his mother finished reading, Jim asked, "Mark the passages in the Bible you read every night, so when I'm away, I can read them, too. I will feel like I'm home at those times."

Eliza Garfield smiled; even though Jim liked school, he obviously missed his family.

The next morning, Jim hitched up Mrs. Reed's buggy and brought it to the door. When his mother came out, he bowed low and said, "Your carriage awaits you, ma'am."

Mrs. Garfield put her hands to her face. "But Jim, we always walk to meetin' on Sunday. What will folks say?"

"Who cares what folks say?" Jim laughed. He helped his mother into the buggy, and Tom climbed up beside him.

As they drove along, Mrs. Garfield asked, "Have you been goin' to meetin' on Sunday, Jim?"

"Yes, mother. We're required to attend every Sunday mornin'. Heard a Mr. Higby preach last week. The other students tell me we have many different preachers, although Professor Branch, the head of the school, often preaches himself."

After meeting and noon dinner were over, Mrs. Garfield packed the buggy with a barrel of flour, more hams and bacon, sugar, and a little tea. Then Jim drove back to Chester with provisions for the remainder of the term. In his pocket he had a dollar and a half of the original seventeen.

14

FIFTY CENTS A DAY

THE REMAINDER OF JIM'S first term at the academy went by quickly as his studies became his life. During the month between spring and fall terms, Jim worked at small carpentry jobs and helped with three days of haying. Never once did he suggest returning to the canal. There wasn't time before the new term began in August, he told himself.

Most of the money he earned, he gave to his mother. During the next term, he worked part-time for a carpenter named Woodworth, who also gave him room and board.

But the fall term would end the last of October. Jim could not return to the canal then, and he had four months before the spring term began in March. Nor could he earn money doing extra jobs around the farms. Most of that work was done between March, when plowing and planting began, and the end of October, when the harvesting was completed.

But winter was also the time when farm children received their schooling. Even the smallest hands were needed earlier. Then young boys had to swing scythes to mow the hay, girls had to pick fruit, and little folks had to hoe long rows of corn. But now the ground was frozen, and the trees were bare. What schooling the farm children received would be crammed into the next four months. And they would be taught by students from the academy like Jim, whose only way to earn money during the winter recess was to teach.

On Friday, October 12, William and Jim went home to Orange, even though the fall term still had more than two weeks left. The next Monday, they walked to Cleveland to be examined by Mr. J. Litch, district director of education, to see if they knew enough reading, writing, and arithmetic to teach.

"Come on, Jim, we gotta hurry if we're gonna get to the examiner's house," William Boynton said as they walked down the muddy streets. "Let's get it over with."

"I'm comin'. I just wanted to see the new railroad station."

"You can see that anytime," William snapped back.

"Oh, yeah? When did you ever see a railroad

station before?" Jim stopped to confront William. "You never saw one. I saw them in Pittsburgh, but this is Cleveland's first one."

"We'll look at the station after the examinations. I don't wanna clutter my head up with anythin' else," William insisted.

"All right," Jim said. "But I'm gonna look at the new buildings afterward. You can walk home by yourself," Jim added to emphasize his intent.

"We're gonna stay at Uncle Thomas's in Newburgh tonight, so we'll have plenty of time to look—later! Now come on."

Despite William's nervousness, both cousins passed the examinations, which were quite simple. They left Mr. Litch's office with new teacher's certificates in their hands.

"Now can we look?" Jim asked.

William was relieved. "All you want. Just so we get to Uncle Thomas's by suppertime."

Jim inspected the train station being built down on the lakefront with a carpenter's eye: it was over two stories high and all brick! Another sign of progress was the construction of a gas works. *Yes,* Jim thought with satisfaction, *Cleveland is catching up to Pittsburgh.*

But William was not impressed. "What's so great about a gas works?"

"If you had ever been to Pittsburgh, you'd know. They have gas lights that shine in the streets at night. Had 'em for years," Jim bragged.

Now Jim headed down to the river and the wharves. He went up and down looking for boat names and people he might know. William tagged along; he had what he came to Cleveland for. Then Jim cut across the neck of land that made the Cuyahoga bend to the canal basin. He looked around for the *Evening Star* to say hello to Ikey, Cook, and even Dave.

As he walked, Jim resumed the gait he had learned to keep himself from being flipped overboard when the *Star* lurched. He looked at the canallers he passed to see if their faces were familiar. And they glanced back—suspiciously, hostilely. Despite his gait and manner, no one recognized him as a canaller. *Has it only been a little more than a year?* Jim wondered.

"Come on, Jim, it's gettin' dark. We gotta get to Uncle Thomas's," William called.

"I'm comin', Willie," Jim answered sadly. Somehow his life on the canal seemed to be over.

Instead of returning by the trail road they had come on, Jim and William paid five cents each to walk the new plank road to Newburgh. Wagons and buggies passed by briskly—no lurching, breaking, or being mired in mud. Yes, indeed, Cleveland was becoming a city.

The next day, Jim and William dressed in their best clothes to apply at the country schools. They had no list of schools needing teachers. All schools needed them, because none employed the same teacher more than one winter.

As they walked along the trail, they discussed where they should apply. "Wait till the school directors find out I'm not eighteen," Jim worried. "No doubt you'll get the job." He was prepared to meet rebuffs.

When they reached Chagrin Falls, Jim and William asked where the director of the school might be found. They were sent to see the president of the bank, which was the only brick building in the village. Trying to look scholarly in their homespun, they approached Mr. Johnson—bank president, teller, and only employee.

"Mr. Johnson?" William began. "I'm William Boynton, and this is my cousin, James Garfield. We're students at Geauga Academy. I've come to apply for a position as a teacher."

"You foreigners?" Mr. Johnson bellowed.

"What?" Even William was surprised by Johnson's abruptness.

"Cain't you hear? No good teachin' if you cain't hear."

"I can hear," William asserted, regaining his composure. "No, we're not foreigners."

"Good. Had a Scotsman in here last year, and none of the kids could understand him. Had to fire him after a week." Johnson paused to glance at their appearance, "Got a certificate?"

"Yes sir—right here," William said as he unfolded the stiff paper.

Jim wanted to leave. Bank president or not, Johnson was talking down to them. Maybe William wanted this job, but Jim would not work here.

Johnson looked William over with tight, pinched eyes. He tried to do the same to Jim, but Jim held Johnson's eyes with his own, the way he had learned to stare bullies down on the canal. No backwoodsman was looking him over like he was a horse for sale.

"I'll take you, not him," Johnson finally said to William. "Pays fifty cents a day, and room and board. Take it or leave it."

"I'll take it," William said eagerly.

"Start in two weeks. You board with a different family each week. Tell me when you get here. Good day." Johnson abruptly dismissed them.

Back outside, William whistled merrily. "What luck!" he said. "Now, Jim, we'll get you a job."

But Jim was irritated by the treatment they had just received. If Mr. Johnson was like most school directors, Jim would rather face them alone.

"Willie, no point you missin' school anymore. You go on back to the academy. I'll be back when I've got a position."

Jim spent the night at his sister's. Neither Hettie nor her husband had kind words for Mr. Johnson. Then the next morning, he continued on. But Jim had no luck that day, nor the next, nor the next as he went from Euclid to Bedford to Northfield.

On Saturday, he called on one of the school directors in Solon, a Mr. Herrington. By now Jim's speech about his qualifications was quite convincing.

Mr. Herrington stopped his work at the saw mill he owned and talked to Jim seriously. "You're a big fellow. Ever do much fightin'?"

Jim did not know how to answer a question that seemed so entrapping. "I can take care of myself," he replied. He didn't dare mention his experience on the canal.

"I think you can take care of some others, too." Herrington laughed. "We need a teacher for the school term. Go 'round and see the other directors. They'll wanna meet you."

Jim felt uneasy. Herrington seemed to be looking for more than a schoolmaster. But he had spent a week looking for work, so he could not refuse the opportunity.

He went to see all the men Herrington named. They, too, seemed more interested in his size than his knowledge. Mr. Southwick, the last director, said, "I'll talk to the others, and we'll let you know Monday morning. Fair enough?"

There was nothing Jim could do but agree. He went back to Orange to wait until Southwick knocked at the cabin door.

"Mr. Garfield," Southwick began. "The other directors agree you are the schoolmaster we want. Here is the bargain. You must teach four months for twelve dollars per month, or three months for thirteen dollars a month. Whichever you've a mind. Room and board included."

"Agreed," Jim said unsmilingly as he offered the director his hand.

"Very well, you'll begin boarding at my place. See you Monday, the fifth of November. Good day, Mr. Garfield."

Jim slammed the door after Mr. Southwick. He was not excited about his new position as schoolmaster. He knew there would be trouble. *Never will I seek a position again,* he thought. *From now on, I'll make myself so skilled in whatever I do that those offerin' positions will seek me out. I'll never go beggin' again!*

15

THE SCHOOL ON THE LEDGE

NOW THAT JIM HAD A JOB, he returned to the academy for the remaining week of the fall term. He had to catch up on work he had missed and prepare for final compositions and declamations.

Most students despised declamations. Students gave speeches on assigned subjects before the entire school while teachers graded them on their logic and presentation. But Jim enjoyed arguing his opinions before others, no matter how large the audience. The excellent response he received at this final declamation only heightened his irritation at leaving Geauga Academy for a grubby schoolhouse of reluctant children, who came to school only when they felt like it or could be spared from home.

After the academy closed for the term, he went home to Orange.

He slept only fitfully the night before he left for Solon. He had to wake himself up early so he could walk the four or five miles before school started. Before daylight he slid out of bed and quietly pulled on his boots, pants, and shirt. He wore the best ones he had in order to look as old as possible. His eighteenth birthday was still more than two weeks away.

His mother was already up stirring the fire to fix him a good breakfast. "Don't know how those folks you're gonna be boardin' with set a table," she said. "Better have somethin' extra to eat." Jim remembered she had said the same thing when he went to work for the salter almost a year and a half ago.

When the two sat down to breakfast, Jim asked grumpily, "Why are you smilin' so early in the mornin', mother?"

"Oh, I'm just pleased one of my sons is gonna be a teacher!"

Jim grunted disgustedly. "Anybody can be a teacher, just so long as he knows a little more than the kids he teaches. Folks don't hold teachers in high regard. Don't pay them much, either. I could make more as a carpenter, only there isn't enough work in the winter."

"Don't you say that, James. Teachin' is a noble profession. Jesus was a teacher. Nobody paid him anything, yet he changed the world."

Jim shrugged.

"You got learnin', James, and you're interested

in gettin' more. Folks can lose their money, their land, and even the clothes off their backs. But nobody can take learnin' away from you once you got it."

"I never thought of it that way. I suppose you're right," Jim replied.

"Remember that when you're teachin' those little folks," his mother advised him. "Every day you give them somethin' nobody can take away."

Jim felt a little better. But he had no more time for discussions. He picked up the wooden box he had packed the night before, kissed his mother, and was once again on the rough road that led away from their cabin.

When he arrived in Solon, Mr. Southwick was eating breakfast. Mrs. Southwick, a plump, middle-aged woman, welcomed him and promptly plied him with food. *At least I'll eat well boarding here for a week,* Jim thought.

Soon he and Mr. Southwick were walking toward the school, which was situated on a ledge above the Chagrin River and nicknamed the On-the-Ledge School of District 2.

The school building could not be considered old, because schools had existed in Ohio for only ten to twenty years. But Solon's schoolhouse was obviously an early one. It had windows, but they were not glass, only heavy paper generously greased with pig fat. There was a crude wood floor, which Jim was glad to see, since dirt floors froze in winter and turned to mud when it rained. Around two of the side walls were the students' benches. These were rough, split logs that Jim remembered getting many a splinter from.

In the center of the room stood a raised, round hearth. Above it was an opening in the ceiling for the smoke to go out and the rain to fall in. At the front end was a plank mounted on two trestles and another log bench. This was Jim's desk.

It all looked familiar. But Jim noticed some unusual holes cut into the logs. "What are those for?" he asked Mr. Southwick.

"Oh, don't use them no more. Schoolmaster and some of the older boys and girls used to shoot outta them if Indians attacked," he replied casually. Then he motioned to the heavy box they had brought with them. "These here are the books you'll be using: Bibles, McGuffey readers, Webster's spellers."

"Is that all?" Jim asked wondering about arithmetic books. But the look on Southwick's face kept him from inquiring. Instead he asked, "How many pupils will attend school?"

"Oh, five—maybe twenty-five. Don't rightly know. Some folks around here just don't hold with learning. Afraid their kids will become irreligious or immoral or run away. But most folks send their kids to learn reading and writing, some ciphering if they can spare them."

Jim said nothing.

Mr. Southwick stayed until the scholars arrived, chatting and helping Jim build a fire. There were seven students all under twelve years of age.

"This here is your new schoolmaster, Mr. Garfield, from over to Orange. He's been learning at Geauga Academy, so you pay attention and you'll be smart as him sooner or later. Now say, 'Good morning, Mr. Garfield.' " He paused for the children to parrot him. "That's good. Well, I'll leave you now," he concluded, his duty done for this year.

Then he turned to Jim. "Good luck, Garfield. Know you'll be a fine teacher." Suddenly he lowered his voice. "Say, Garfield, where's your whip?"

"My what?" Jim croaked.

"Your whip. Can't teach school without a whip," Mr. Southwick insisted.

"No teacher ever used a whip on me," Jim argued.

"Look here, Garfield. We hired you, even if you are a mite young, because you looked like you could keep order. Now we expect you to do that."

"I thought I was hired to teach these children somethin'," Jim shot back.

"That, too. But you can't teach them if they're swinging off the rafters. Oh, well, you'll learn." Mr. Southwick left the school.

Jim looked at the seven children. *I couldn't beat those little ones,* he thought. Then he announced, "We'll have our prayers now." He said prayers aloud, and then said a silent one for himself.

Until school was over, the children behaved.

Jim could not believe Mr. Southwick. Until school was dismissed, the children were well behaved.

The next day, eleven students appeared. The original seven had found the new schoolmaster young and inexperienced and reported this to their older brothers and sisters. By noon, the newest scholars agreed. The afternoon session was bedlam. They talked constantly and played games on the benches between them. Jim ended the day feeling very discouraged.

Wednesday began well even though there were now sixteen students. Jim taught the older ones algebra and the young children all levels of arithmetic from the *Ray's Arithmetic Book,* which Mr. Southwick had belatedly found. The same separation was needed for reading. The older students read *Robinson Crusoe* while the younger ones struggled with *McGuffey's First Reader*. Together, the whole class learned geography, history, and grammar from Jim's own books, because the school district considered these subjects unnecessary. With the copybooks their mothers had made by sewing sheets of paper together, all the students sat at the writing table, practicing their *o's* and *l's* with feather quills dipped in crushed berry ink. Frontier people prized reading and writing a fine-looking hand as sufficient education.

While Jim worked with the younger students, the older boys began playing games on the back benches, becoming noisier and noisier.

"Stop that! Get back to your studies now," Jim yelled.

"We're studyin', Jim. Cain't you see? Are you blind?" they shot back, calling him by his first name.

By Thursday morning, Jim had a plan. After opening prayers, he announced, "I'm makin' some changes."

The boys on the back benches smirked.

"Johnny Smith, you go sit on the north-side bench," Jim ordered.

Johnny was so startled he moved immediately.

"Mason, over there, and Huddleston, over here," Jim continued.

The boys did as they were told. This left the big Herrington boy—son of the first director Jim had seen—by himself, which was what Jim wanted.

Thursday and Friday, went better because of the new seating arrangement. And on Saturday, it rained, so fewer students came. By the end of his first week, Jim felt he had established control. Now learning could begin.

16
DECLAMATIONS

TEACHING A FRONTIER SCHOOL was hard work, and Jim was tired at the end of each day. But each evening the different families he boarded with talked more about school or had him tutor their children. Then he returned to school for another day. The tedium would have stifled Jim if he had not organized a debating society, the Philomethian, with friends from Geauga who lived close by in Chagrin Falls.

The society met on Jim's first Saturday night in Solon to debate whether the African race had suffered greater injustice from the whites than the American Indian. Jim was the spokesman for the affirmative.

After the debate, James Hinkley, an observer who was also a teacher at the academy, stood up.

"We are gratified as teachers to see our students

keeping their wits sharp, as some of them sharpen the wits of others. I shall report this to the head of the academy, Professor Branch. Meanwhile, I have an offer to make."

There was a rumble of excitement as the members and their guests wondered what Hinkley was proposing.

Mr. Hinkley continued. "As you may know, I live here in Chagrin Falls. I propose to hold a geography school, consisting of a dozen sessions. Does this interest you?"

The wave of murmurs indicated that it did.

"Very well, then. I will charge fifty cents a person for twelve lessons to be held two evenings a week at my house. The first ones will be next Thursday and Friday."

Jim was the first to sign up and pay his fifty cents. *What I learn I can pass on to my students,* he thought. *Besides, several of my evenings will now be filled.*

Jim looked forward to another week with his students, and he was not disappointed on Monday. School went very well. But on Tuesday, Jim ordered Samuel Herrington to stop kicking the smaller children in front of him.

"I ain't doin' nothin', Jim."

"Mr. Garfield, sir!" Jim ordered.

"I ain't doin' nothin', Jim," he repeated and gave one little boy such a sharp dig with the toe of his boot that the child leaped up, yelping. Then he sat down again, afraid he too might be punished.

"Move to the end of the bench, Samuel," Jim ordered. But Herrington did not move.

With one swift leap, Jim jumped over the front benches, pulled Samuel out of his seat, and threw him across another bench. But he was not going to submit to being caned.

He whipped around and was up on his feet again. "I been waitin' a whole week for this, Mr. Garfield."

Fearful that the small children might be hurt if a fight occurred in the small schoolroom, Jim backed out of the door onto the open ground outside.

Samuel was taunting him, mistaking Jim's movement for a retreat. "I ain't one of the little boys, schoolmaster. I'm a man, bigger than you."

Jim said nothing, so Samuel grabbed for his hair to make him stand still. As he did, Jim punched him in the stomach, followed by a left punch to his jaw. Samuel went sprawling. The smaller children crowded around the door, barely moving. Jim left Samuel gasping for breath and went back into the school as the children scrambled to their seats.

The next day Jim had twenty-five students. He was sure the children had told their parents, who sent their other children once they knew the schoolmaster would enforce discipline. Now Jim instituted a rule that not even whispering would be allowed.

By late November, the winter snows began, and all but routine farm chores ended. Finally the bigger boys began coming to school. By the first week in December, Jim had thirty-seven students some days.

Some of these were the sons of mountain hunters and trappers, who had come into the Ohio forests far in advance of civilization. They had lived with the Iroquois Indians, usually sleeping in the open during summer months and in a cave or wigwam in winter. Often they had married Indian maidens and became almost as much a part of nature as their wives.

Some had moved on when the first forts appeared, but others let civilization catch up with them. They built cabins away from the villages and married hardy white women—usually widows—who kept gardens, cows, pigs, and chickens. The men knew nothing but hunting. They could not read or write and often beat up strangers who could.

Jim had grown up with mountain men and their sons. He knew they prized shooting and fighting above all else. Only their women understood that their boys would live in a future that valued learning, and persuaded them to attend school. Some were eighteen or nineteen, even twenty, years old. And they came to tease the girls and show off in a crude, courting ritual, not to please their mothers.

When they saw that Jim was big and heard

about Herrington, they remained orderly. They were not ready to try the schoolmaster yet. And Jim let them be. They came to class irregularly, and he was too busy to pay much attention to them.

As the short, dark December days dragged on, the children became noisy and restless. School did not even break for Christmas. The people of the Western Reserve did not notice the religious holiday.

The first week in January, Jim ordered Henry Dunwell to read in front of the class. Henry had been trying to get Jane Smith's attention. Now that he had done so, he would not be distracted.

"I'm busy," he answered. Jane Smith turned bright red and covered her face with her apron.

"Henry! Get up here!" Jim commanded.

"You read it. You read a sight better'n me anyhow." The children and big girls snickered, and the boys watched with interest.

Jim pulled Henry out of his seat. "Get up and read!"

But Henry grabbed a length of kindling from the hearth and came at Jim.

"Ain't you forgettin' the code of frontier fightin'?" Jim taunted. "No weapons. Just fists." Jim grabbed Henry's arm and swung him around. The wooden club fell.

But Henry was not subdued. Both young men moved around the fire on the raised hearth. Jim saw no way to get Henry outside. Anyway, gossip had probably spread that trick around.

Jim baited Henry as far from the other children as possible. Then he stood perfectly still and let Henry come for him.

As Henry leaped forward, Jim grabbed his shirt and threw him against the front wall of the schoolhouse. But Henry was back on Jim, scratching and kicking. Jim brought his knee up hard into Henry's stomach. "Think you can beat a canaller, huh, mountain boy?" he snarled.

Doubled over with pain, Henry Dunwell, Jr., escaped out the schoolhouse door.

While Jim caught his breath, the students were strangely quiet: they had not known their schoolmaster was a canaller.

Late that night, Jim lay in the loft of the tinker's house thinking about his encounter with Henry. Here he was using the tricks he learned on the canal to teach school. He knew he should be helping his scholars, not fighting with them.

He thought about each student that came to school regularly. Johnny Smith needed work in spelling. And Margaret could not get the idea of ciphering. If she were left a widow like his mother, she could not take care of selling land or paying debts.

Jim went on thinking about each of his students and their individual needs. Maybe if they were interested in their studies, they would be less inclined to get into mischief, he concluded as he resolved to do better from then on.

Jim could have ended school the first of February, because his bargain with the directors had been for three months, only four if he wanted to continue. But Jim was beginning to enjoy teaching.

After prayers one morning Jim addressed the class. "We have only four weeks of school left," he began, but was interrupted by cheers from the students. He went on. "I think we ought to show our families and friends how much progress we've made. Therefore, we're gonna spend the time left preparin' declamations, which we will invite parents and friends to hear on the last day of class. The smallest children will read from their readers or the Bible. Older students will prepare their own recitations on somethin' they have learned. I'll be around to help each of you."

Jim began with the four- to-seven year olds. Some of them could hardly talk well. After a while, he had adjusted to their speech and gestures, but how would visitors understand them? At least they might learn something as they prepared.

The older children could choose to read, cipher, or write. Two ten-year-old girls approached his desk timidly and asked if they might do something together. Jim knew they were too shy to do anything alone, so he helped them select a story from the Bible to dramatize.

But he was most surprised when Samuel Herrington approached. Since the day Jim had knocked him down, he had been fairly well behaved.

"Mr. Garfield, I'd like to read the Declaration of Independence. I was tellin' my folks about it when you read it to us. They didn't know much about it," he explained. "I sure would feel mighty good if I could read it outta your book. Would you let me borrow it?"

Jim was pleased. "I'll bring the book tomorrow so you can practice, Samuel. That's a splendid idea." Samuel nodded and went back to his seat.

The last day of school was Saturday, March 2. In the morning, the students rehearsed their recitations, dressed in the best clothes they had—some store-bought, some homespun. Their faces and hands were the cleanest Jim had seen in four months. For the shy ones, it was a painful experience. For others, it was, at last, an approved way of showing off.

In the afternoon, one hundred people squeezed into the log schoolhouse—parents, grandparents, sisters, and brothers. Some had walked miles in the driving March wind. All were farmers or townspeople except one man in fringed buckskin: a mountain man who came to hear his son read, a skill the father never had.

All the parents seemed proud that their children had been taught something; they clapped at every child's efforts, no matter how stumbling.

Jim wished he had realized they really cared about education. He would have tried harder. As he listened to each boy and girl, he was both proud and ashamed. The fault did not lie with these struggling people or their children. It was he who lacked the insight to see their real potential.

As the students left, he stood at the door, speaking a word of encouragement to each one. When they had all gone, he put out the fire, locked the door, and walked home to the cabin at Orange once more.

17

ONE FOOT ON THE ROAD

THAT EVENING WHEN SUPPER WAS OVER, Jim and his mother sat before the glowing fire. Jim could tell his mother was lonely now that Tom had married and moved away.

Jim wished he could see his own future in the surging blaze. When he was a boy and looked into the fire, he had seen all sorts of pictures. Now all he saw were orange and blue flames.

"What's the matter, James? I thought you would be glad to be home for a few days," his mother said a little worried.

Jim managed to smile. "I am, mother—real glad."

"Well, you sure don't look happy. You just finished your first teaching job. Now you'll go back to the academy and get more learnin'. You got a good future," she said encouragingly.

"Do I, mother?" Jim shook his head. "I just don't seem to be headed anywhere. What am I meant to be? I wanted to be a sailor for the longest time. Then I thought I could be a teacher. But I didn't teach those younguns much." He paused to think further. "I should be home workin' the farm, instead of takin' money from you and spendin' it on school."

"James," his mother said sternly, "I want you to go to school. You do fine there, and I'm proud of you. I gotta agree that you ain't meant to be a farmer. Mind you, farmin' is a good life. But for you, James, there are other things."

"What other things?" Jim demanded.

"We don't always know what the Lord wants us to do. But trust him, and he'll show you the way," his mother pleaded.

Jim thought about what his mother was saying. He remembered how she had prayed for him when he seemed to be dying of ague. And he remembered that rainy night he fell into the canal, when only a crack in the boat's deck had kept him from drowning. Maybe if he had paused to think longer that night, he would not have stayed on the canal and gotten sick. But if God was trying to guide him, where was he leading?

"James," his mother broke into his thoughts. "Tomorrow starts a whole week of meetin's—days and evenin's—at the schoolhouse. Elder William A. Lillie is goin' to conduct them. Maybe the meetin's will help you," Mrs. Garfield said hopefully.

When Jim came down from the loft Sunday morning, his mother was already stirring a cooking iron full of eggs and bacon while the black teakettle steamed over the fire.

"Mother, you look like you're goin' to a party instead of a meetin'," Jim said as they ate breakfast.

"Elder Lillie makes folks understand the Lord's word like no one else. Yes sir, this is a week I look forward to." Eliza's hand hit the wooden table for emphasis. "Now quit your dallyin' and eat."

Jim just laughed. When she was excited, his mother always talked to him as if he were a small boy.

Because they arrived at the meeting early, Jim and his mother got front-row seats. But Eliza soon made Jim give his up to a latecomer who was standing. Jim joined the other young men leaning against the back wall as Elder Lillie began to speak. He was a large man whose store-bought clothes did not hide the weathered face and rough hands that marked a frontiersman.

"Welcome, friends. We meet under this simple roof to praise God. When Jesus spoke here on earth, he did not even have a simple structure like this. He spoke out-of-doors under the great canopy of God's blue sky. I always feel his presence there, and I know you do, too."

Jim thought about the times he had stood on a rise and looked at the reach of forests and meadows touching the sky. He, too, felt close to his Creator at those times.

Then Elder Lillie began to speak of God's plan for all to live in harmony. But people did not live this way. They were headstrong and willful, leading them to feel fearful, discouraged, confused, and unhappy.

Jim nodded in agreement. That was just the way he felt lately.

Lillie said that God gave us a choice so we could live as we wished. But we were at peace only when we were living as God wanted us to. Then Lillie spoke of a way to live God's plan—a way every person could find for himself by knowing Jesus Christ. He spoke in terms the pioneers understood. He told them the way to know Christ was clearly marked in the words of the Bible. The gospel was their map and the Holy Spirit their guide if they would let themselves be guided.

Jim nodded his head again. When he heard preachers speak, he always tested what they said against the Scriptures he knew. What Elder Lillie said seemed right.

"Come forward and accept the Christian life," Lillie urged as he closed his message. "Be baptized and washed clean of your sins. Then set your foot upon the road the gospel has paved. That road will lead you to peace."

Jim was startled when a friend of his rose and went forward. He watched as the young man and Elder Lillie talked.

When the meeting was over, Jim went home, wondering if the way was as clearly marked as Lillie had said. He spent the afternoon studying the Bible.

In the evening, Elder Lillie spoke again. Jim listened, and as he listened, he understood. The real truth was in Jesus Christ. If Jim followed Christ's example, his life would never be false or meaningless.

When Elder Lillie finished his address, he said again: "Come forward. Begin a new life. Obey the gospel."

This time, Jim rose and went forward.

Elder Lillie talked to Jim quietly, and then he said, "Prepare yourself in these hours of darkness. In the first light of day, you will be baptized to walk in the newness of life."

All night Jim sat by the firelight reading. His mother said nothing to him. She knew the words Jim read that evening would influence his entire future.

On Monday morning, March 4, 1850, Jim met Elder Lillie by the creek that ran past their cabin. As his mother, Aunt Alpha and Uncle Amos Boynton, his cousins, and neighbors watched, Elder Lillie led Jim into the creek. Patches of ice floated here and there, but Jim did not feel the cold.

Gently, William Lillie supported Jim as he laid him back in the water until he was completely submerged. Then Lillie spoke, "I baptize you in the name of the Father, Son, and Holy Spirit for the remission of your sins." He lifted Jim back up as if he were a small child.

Each day more people laid down their work and came to hear this preacher. On the last day, Sunday, March 10, the little schoolhouse was filled.

"Folks, I think you've heard enough of my old voice this week," Elder Lillie began—but shouts of "no" muffled his next words. He smiled and held up his hands. "As you know, it is our custom to let folks speak their feelings about the Lord at our meetings. Now I would like to call on the people who decided to accept the Christian life this week. Tell us how God came into your lives these past few days."

There was an expectant silence as people turned their heads to see who would step forward.

"Come, folks. Don't keep the joy to yourselves. Give others a glimpse of the light you have seen."

One girl put her hands up to her scarlet face, and a man grasped the edge of the rough bench as if to keep from jumping up. Finally, Jim stood up. He did not know what he would say, but he knew the words would come.

Elder Lillie beckoned him to the front of the log room and patted him gently on the back. Jim looked down at the rough puncheon floor before he lifted his head and began to speak.

"This week seventeen people have been baptized. . . . As you know, I was one of them. About six months ago I was taken with the ague in Cleveland. When I consider what has happened since, I know God has been guiding my life.

"When I was a canaller, I was exposed to every type of vice. But before I could adopt these ways, I was taken sick and was unable to do heavy work for months. So I went to the academy to occupy my mind. Soon I realized that life there was more stimulating than the canal had ever been. Now I thank God that I am what I am, and not a sailor.

"I don't know where my craving for learnin' will lead me. But now I can trust God to make the best of my life. Only he knows what that will be."

Jim walked slowly back to his rough-hewn seat. He was no longer worried about his future; he would listen to the stirrings within him and the counsel he received from Scripture. With God's help, anything was possible. . . .

Epilogue

JAMES GARFIELD'S EXPERIENCE on March 4, 1850, guided the rest of his life. His Christian belief and native determination brought him to great accomplishments—teacher, preacher, legislator, general, congressman, lawyer, and finally, president of the United States.

On Tuesday, March 12, Jim and his cousin William returned to Geauga Academy. After two more terms, Jim realized he wanted more education than the academy offered. He taught school and worked as a carpenter to earn the money to attend Western Reserve Electic Institute at Hiram, Ohio, a school Elder William Lillie and others had founded. Here Jim became well known as a preacher because of his strong belief in God and his forceful way of speaking.

After two years at the institute, Jim wanted to

attend college. He took a qualifying examination from Williams College in New Hampshire and was granted admission as a junior. When he graduated in 1856, he returned to the Western Reserve Electic Institute to teach Greek, Latin, English, literature, grammar, geology, and other subjects. Sometimes he taught six or seven classes a day starting at five o'clock in the morning. In two years, he became head of the Institute, which he expanded into a noteworthy school on the junior college level.

During all this time, Garfield was well known as an evangelist. When he preached, men, women, and children came forward to be baptized. In 1858, he is said to have preached twenty-seven times in twenty-seven days.

In November of that year, he married Lucretia Rudolph, the girl he had met nine years earlier at Geauga Academy. They had seven children, but two of them died young. Garfield remained devoted to his mother and often asked her advice. But he did not always do as she wished. His mother was opposed to his becoming involved in politics or joining the army.

But he became a supporter of the newly organized Republican party, and by 1859 he was elected to the Ohio legislature. When the Civil War broke out, he helped recruit a regiment for the Union side and became its colonel. Some of the soldiers were his former students.

During a campaign in the Sandy Valley in Kentucky, he saved his troops, who were trapped in a sudden flood, by piloting a boat down the raging river. As a result, he won a battle that drove the Confederates out of that part of Kentucky.

In the Battle of Chickamauga, Garfield made a dangerous ride under enemy fire to inform other Union generals that the Confederates had broken through Union lines.

Meanwhile, the people of Ohio elected him to Congress, and he took his seat there in December 1863. Later, he became leader of his party in the House of Representatives and in 1880 was elected to the United States Senate.

But the Republicans that year could not settle on a candidate for president. The convention became hopelessly deadlocked between James G. Blaine and Ulysses S. Grant. On the thirty-sixth ballot, they finally agreed on a compromise candidate; his name was James Abram Garfield.

He won the election, and when he was sworn in as the twentieth president of the United States, he leaned over to kiss a tiny, white-haired woman who sat near him—his mother.

James Garfield had been in office four months when he was shot by Charles Julius Guiteau, a man who had been turned down for a government job. The bullets did not hit any of Garfield's vital organs. If he had been shot today, he would have recovered quickly. But he died eighty days later on

September 29, 1881—not of the bullets, but from the infection they created. One of his doctors was his cousin Silas Boynton. Eliza Garfield outlived her son by seven years—a son who once wrote: "Reviewed my strange, strange life and pondered the why: why have I thus been spared, and brought up from the dark deep pits. God only knows. May I obey His precepts, be His child indeed—and let His will lead on and mark the pathway of my chequered life."